This book belongs to

....

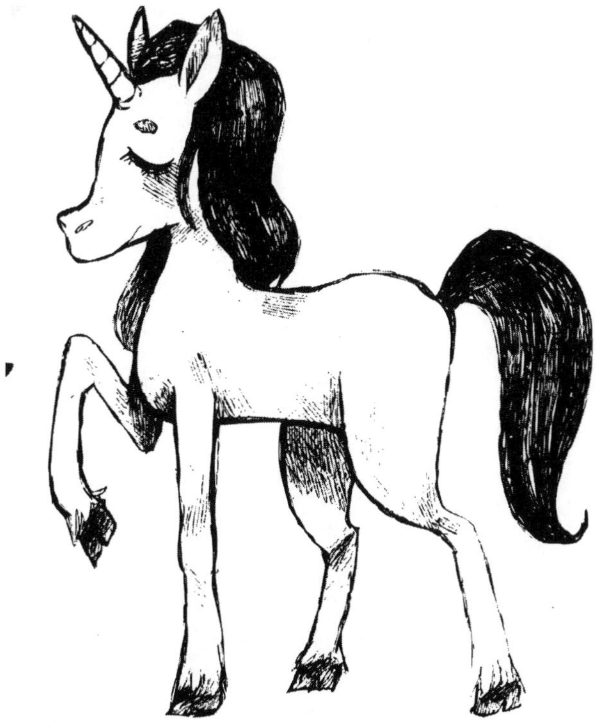

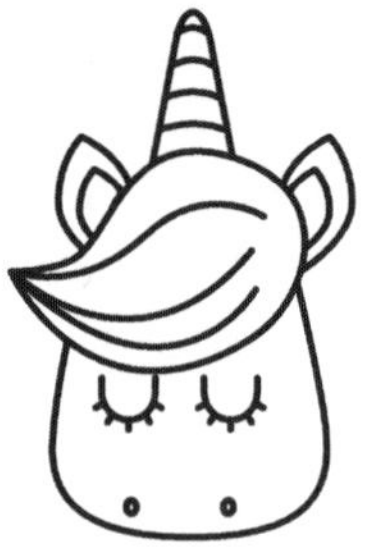

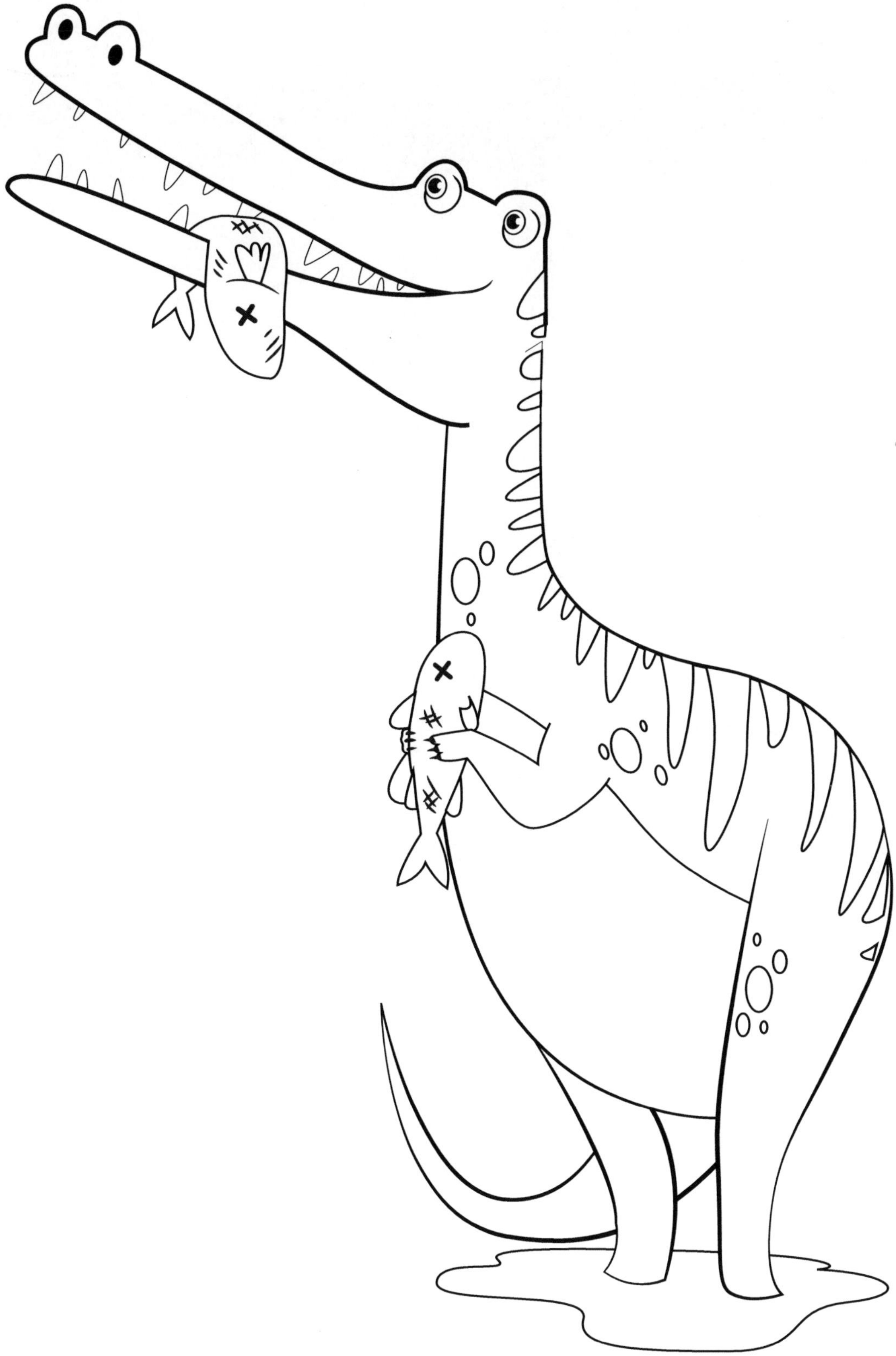

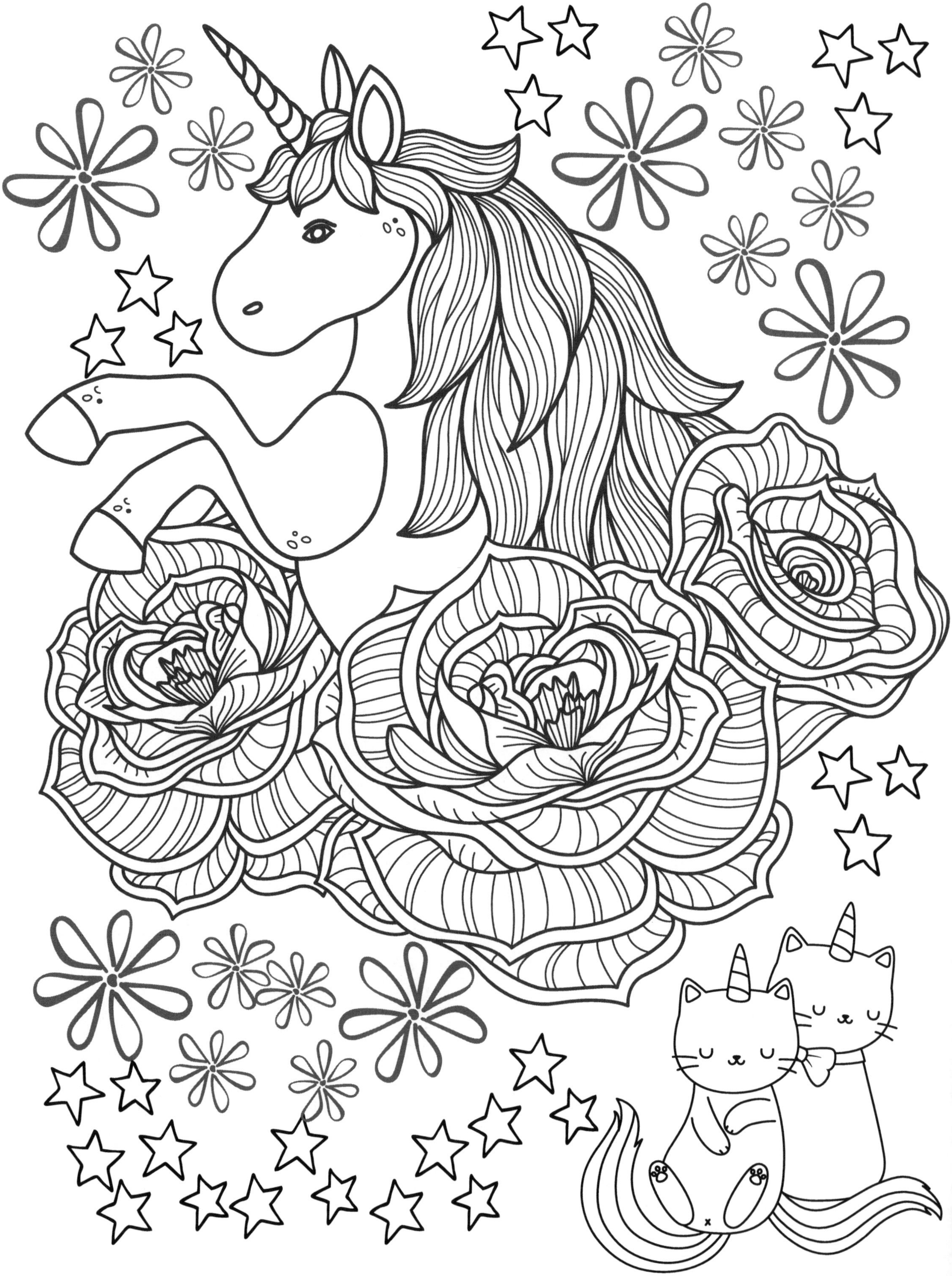

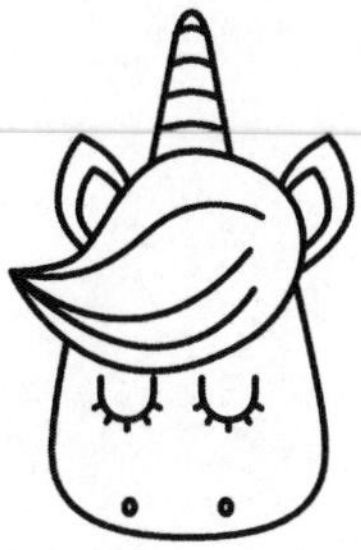

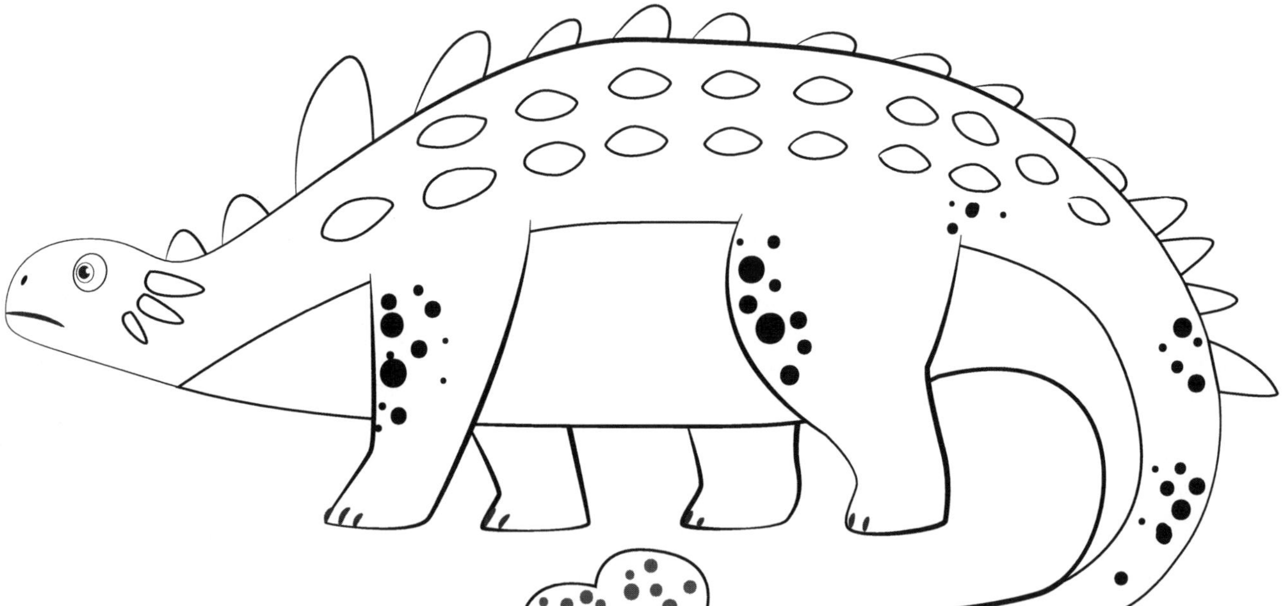

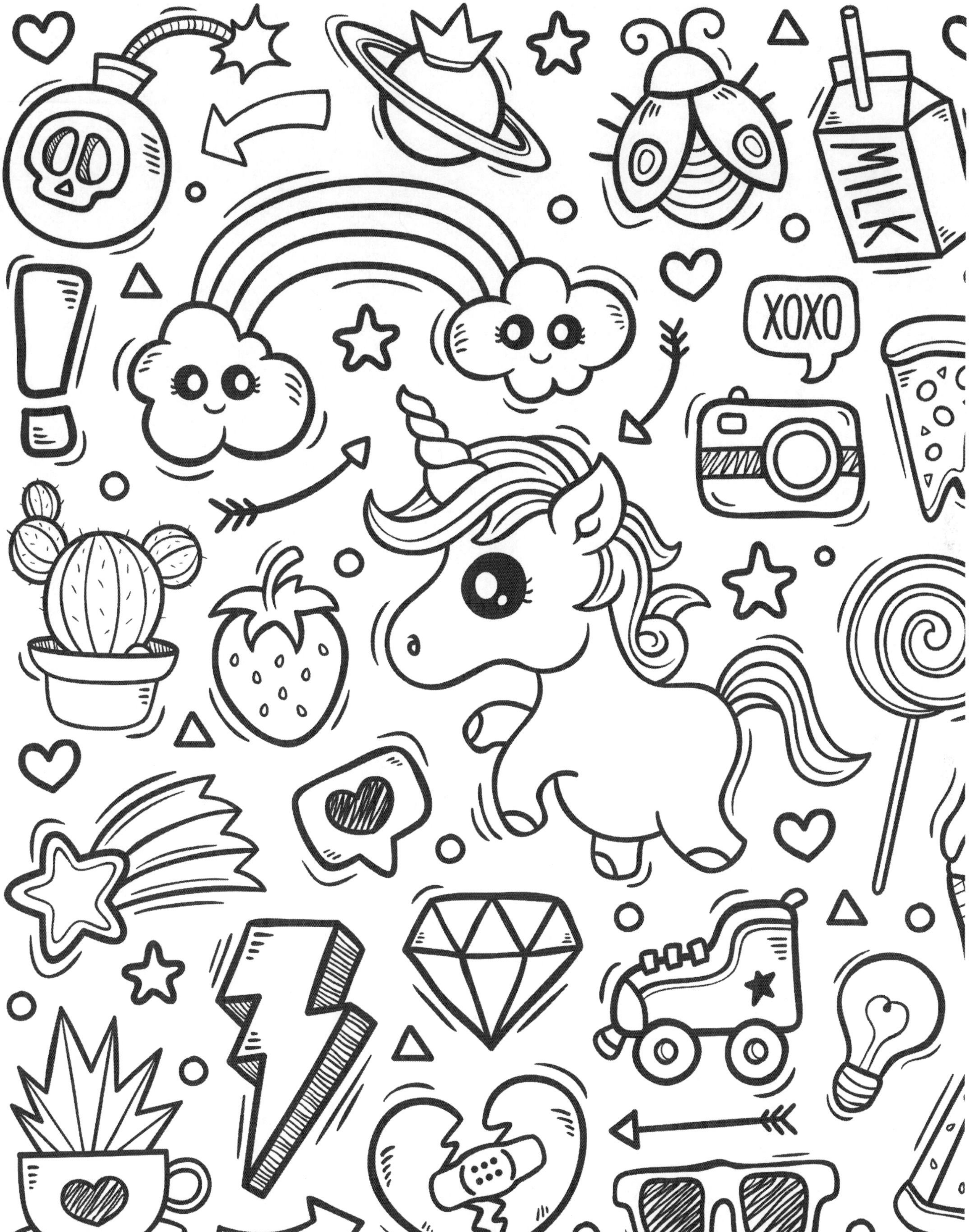
MILK
XOXO

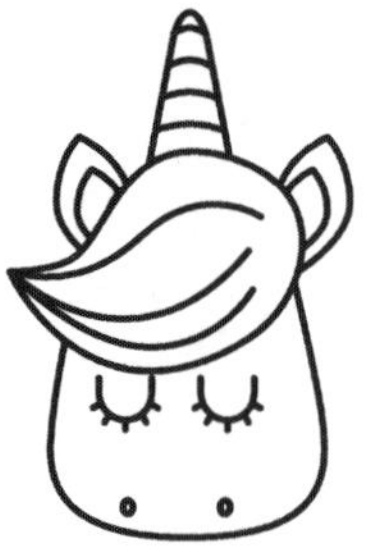

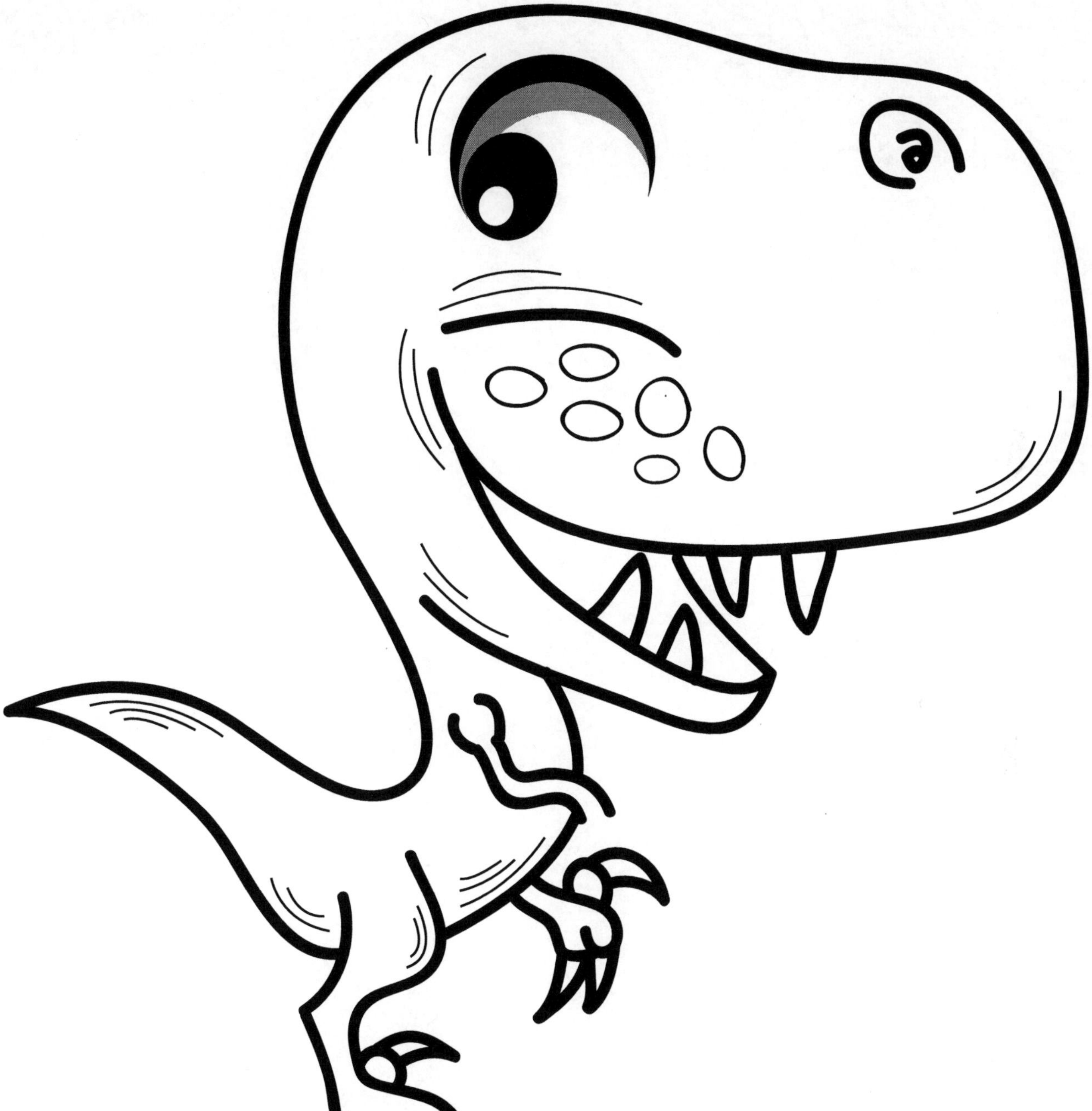

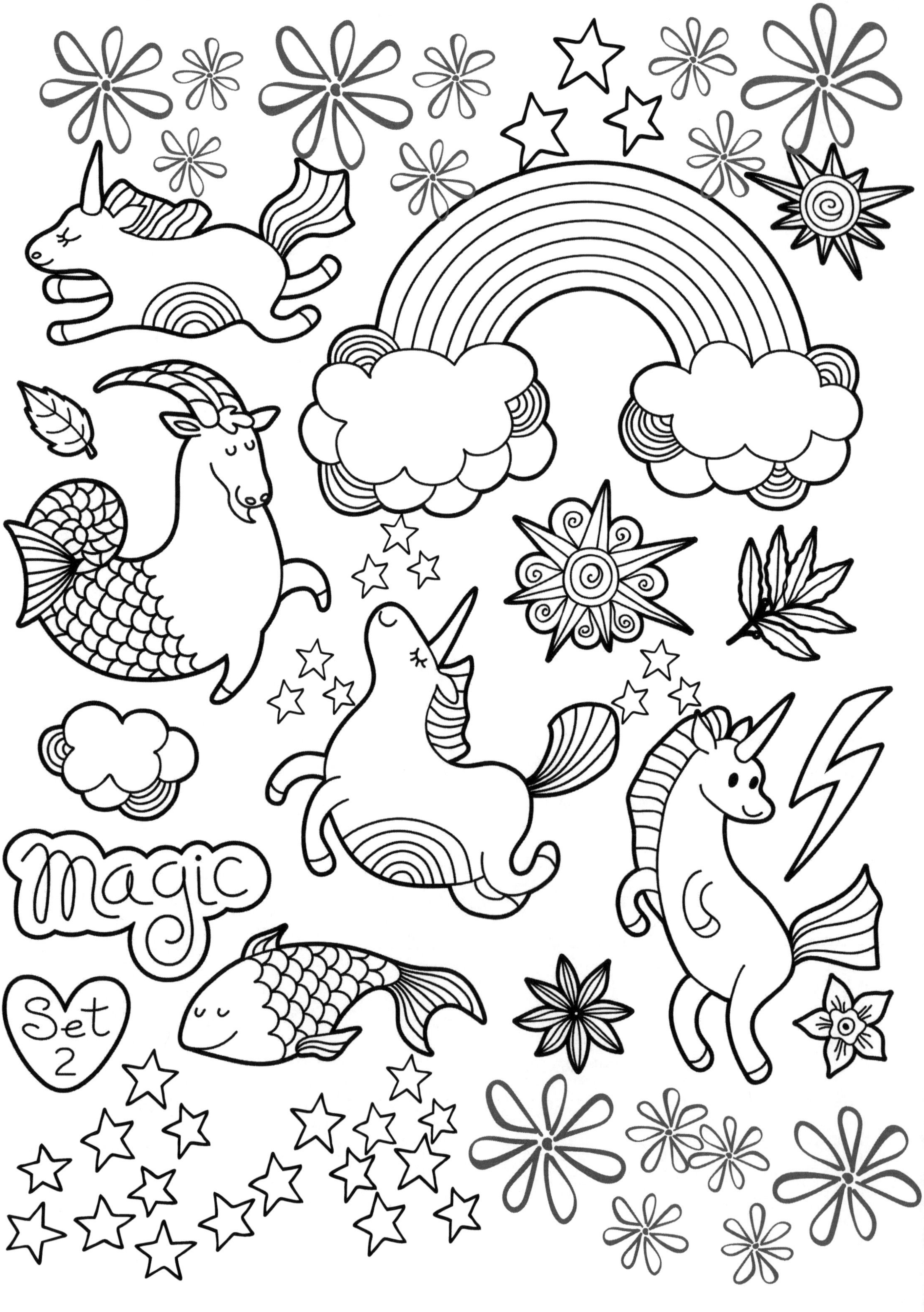
Magic
Set 2

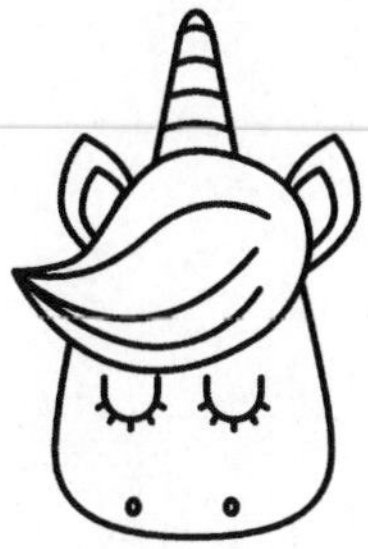

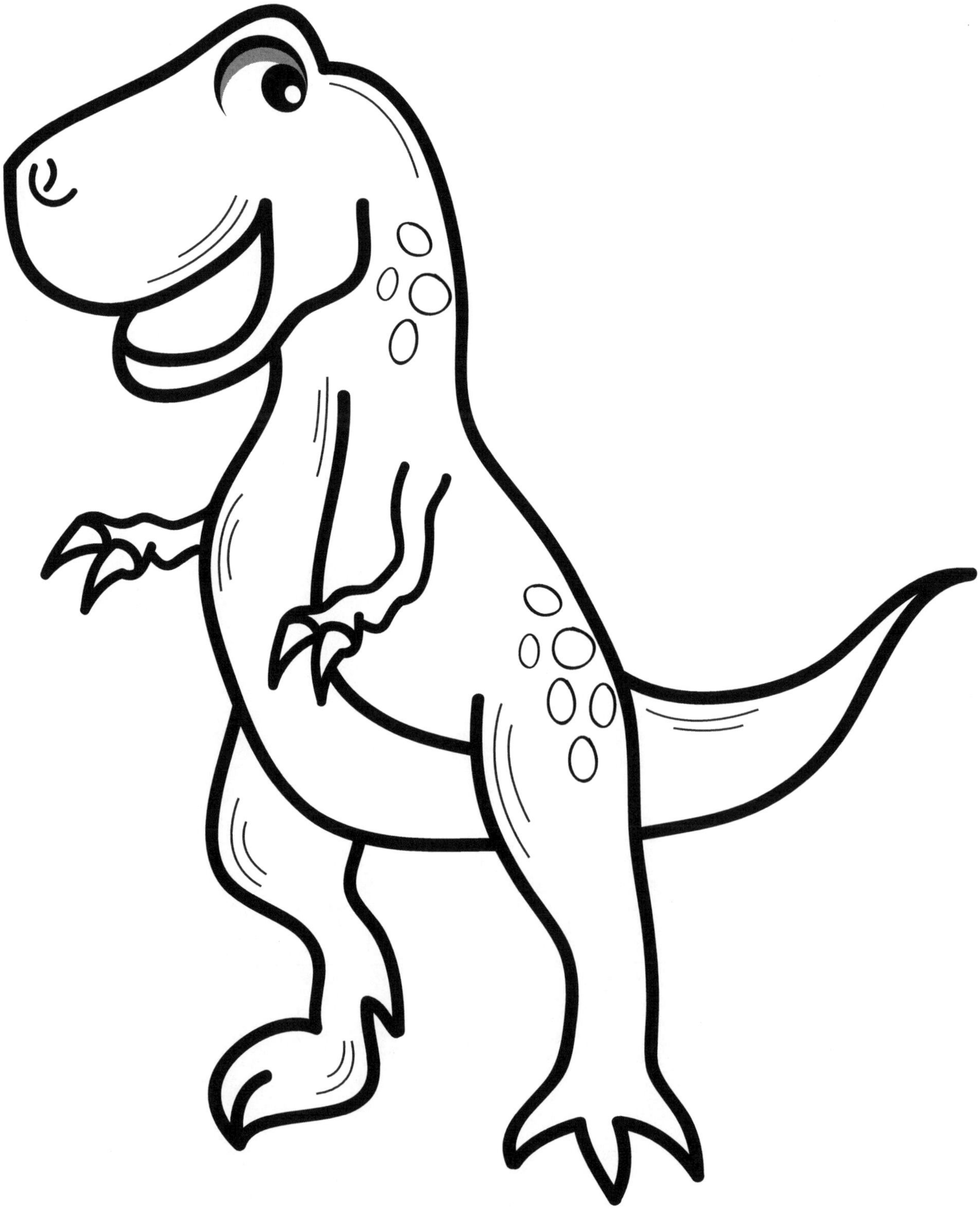

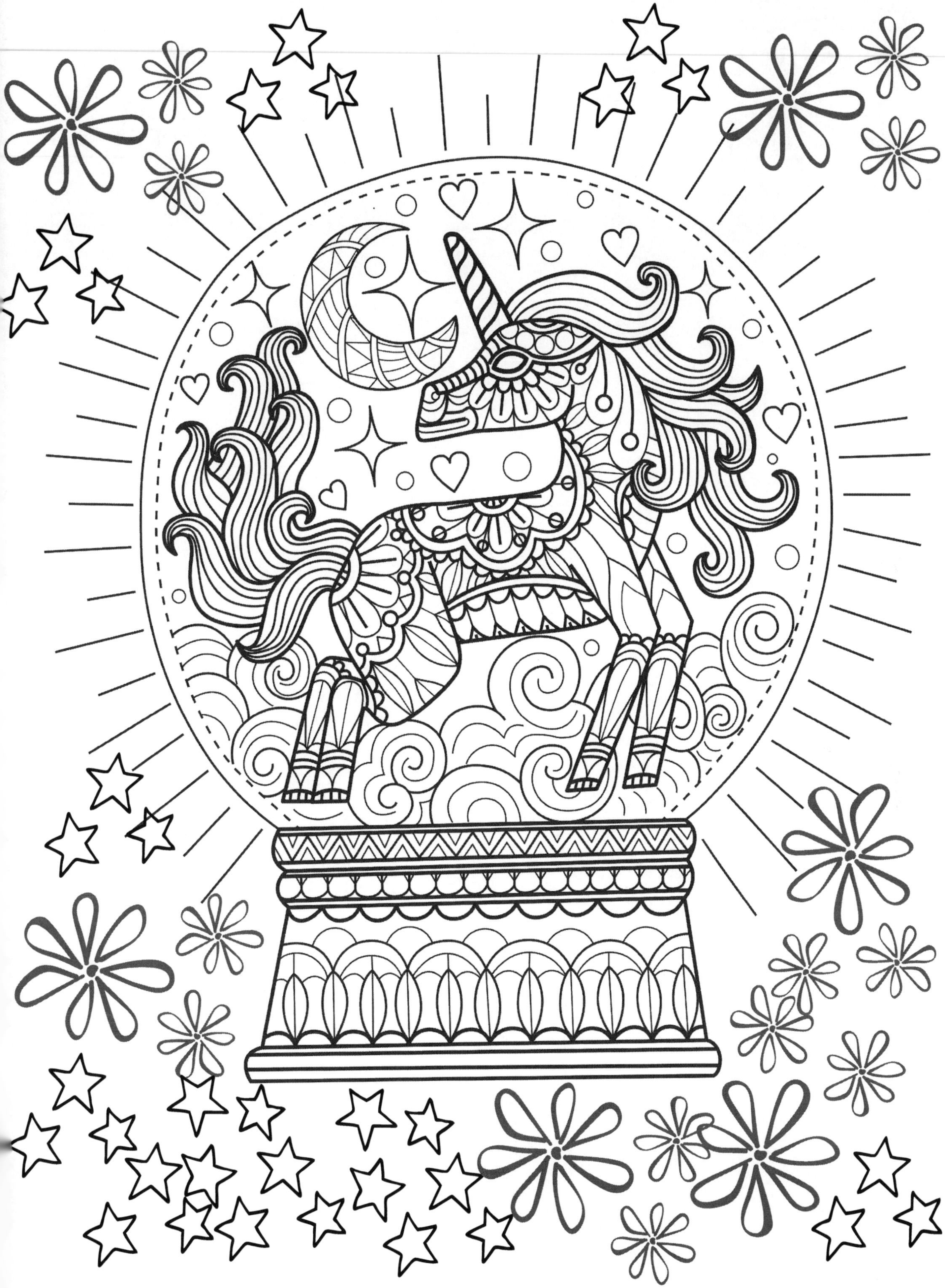

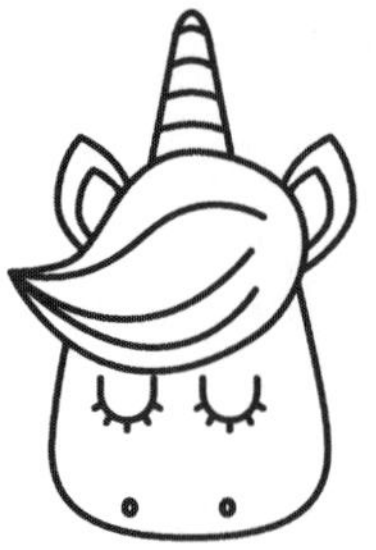

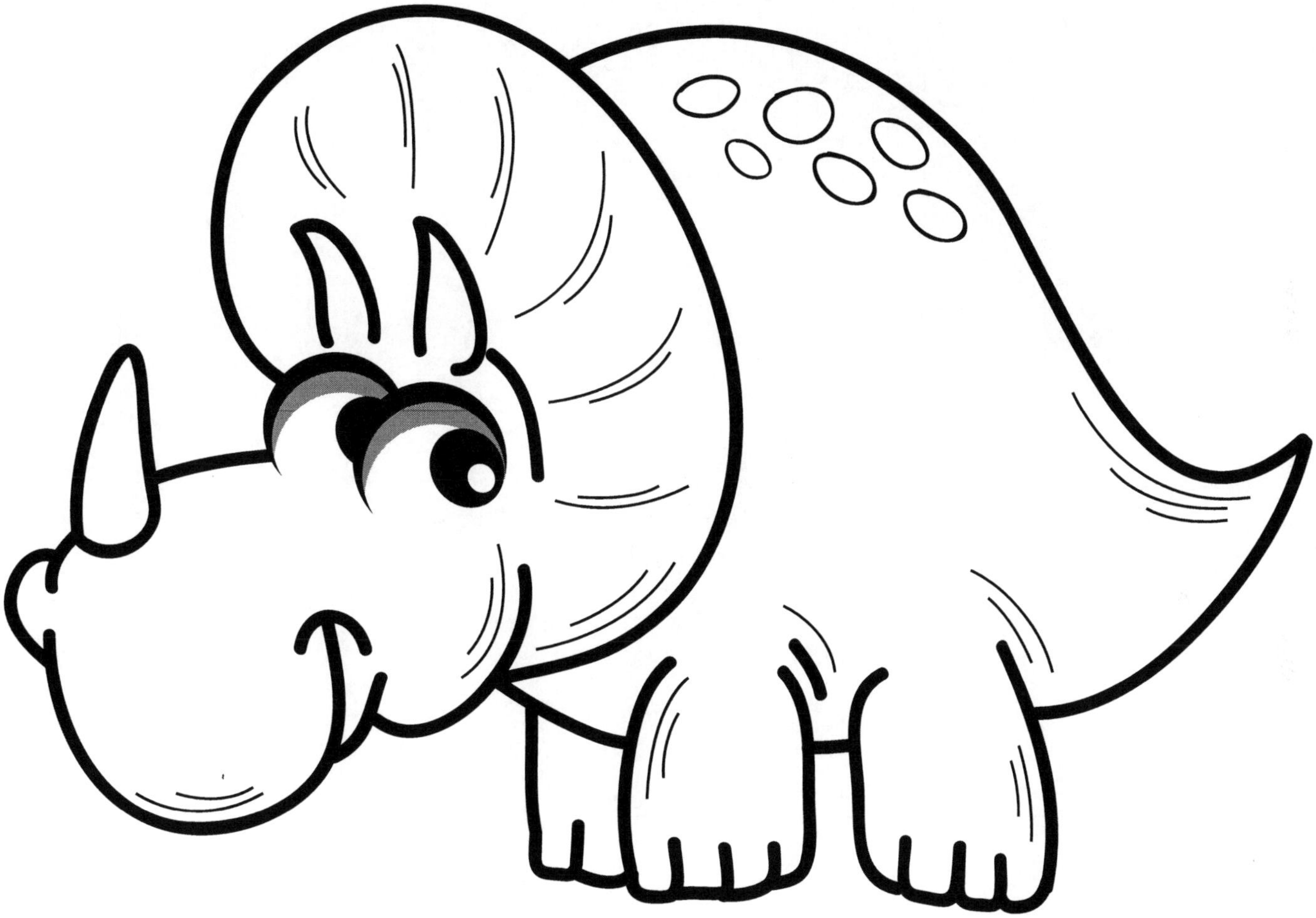

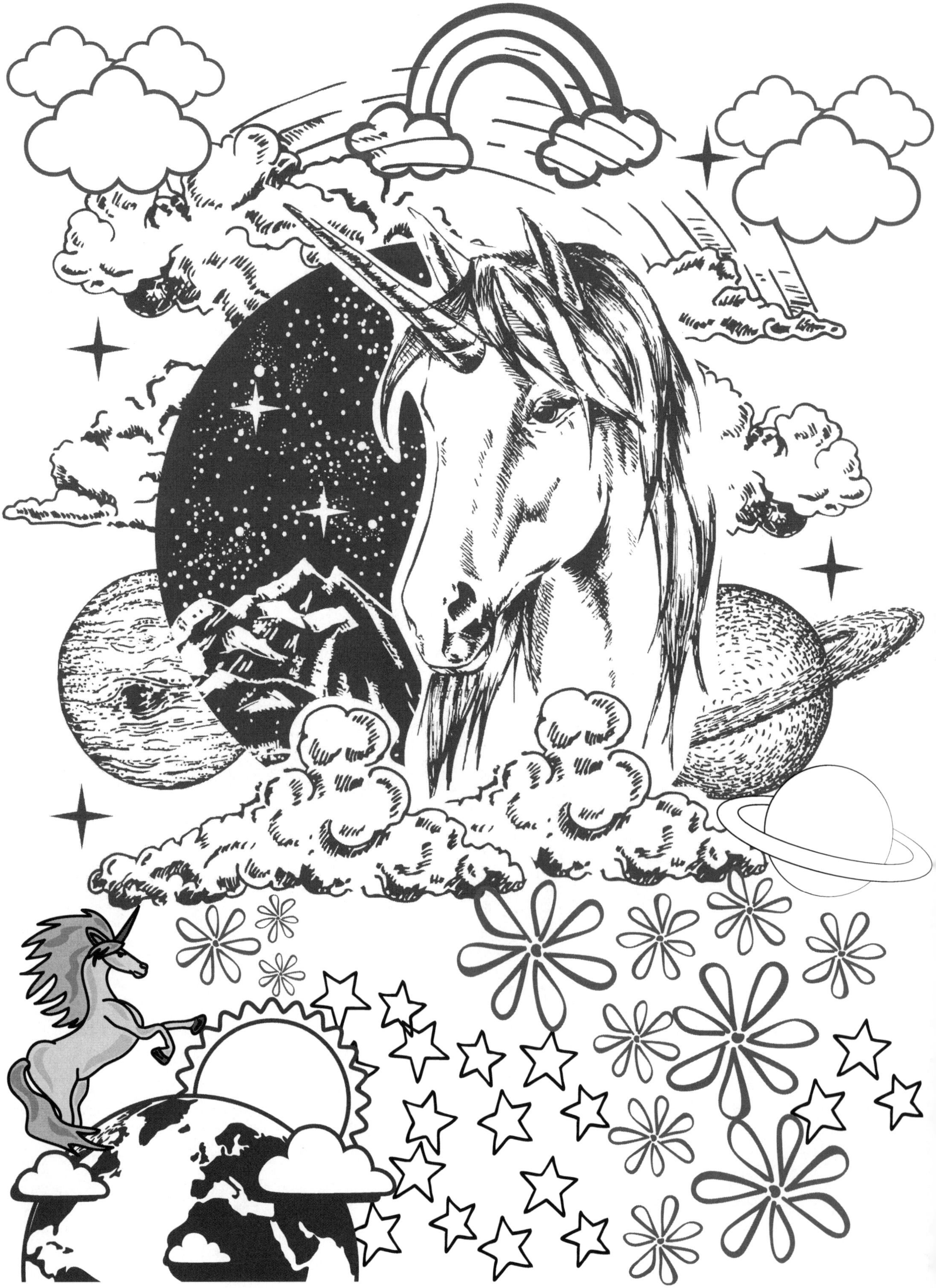

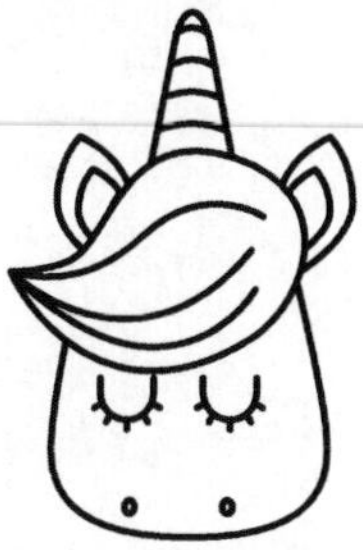

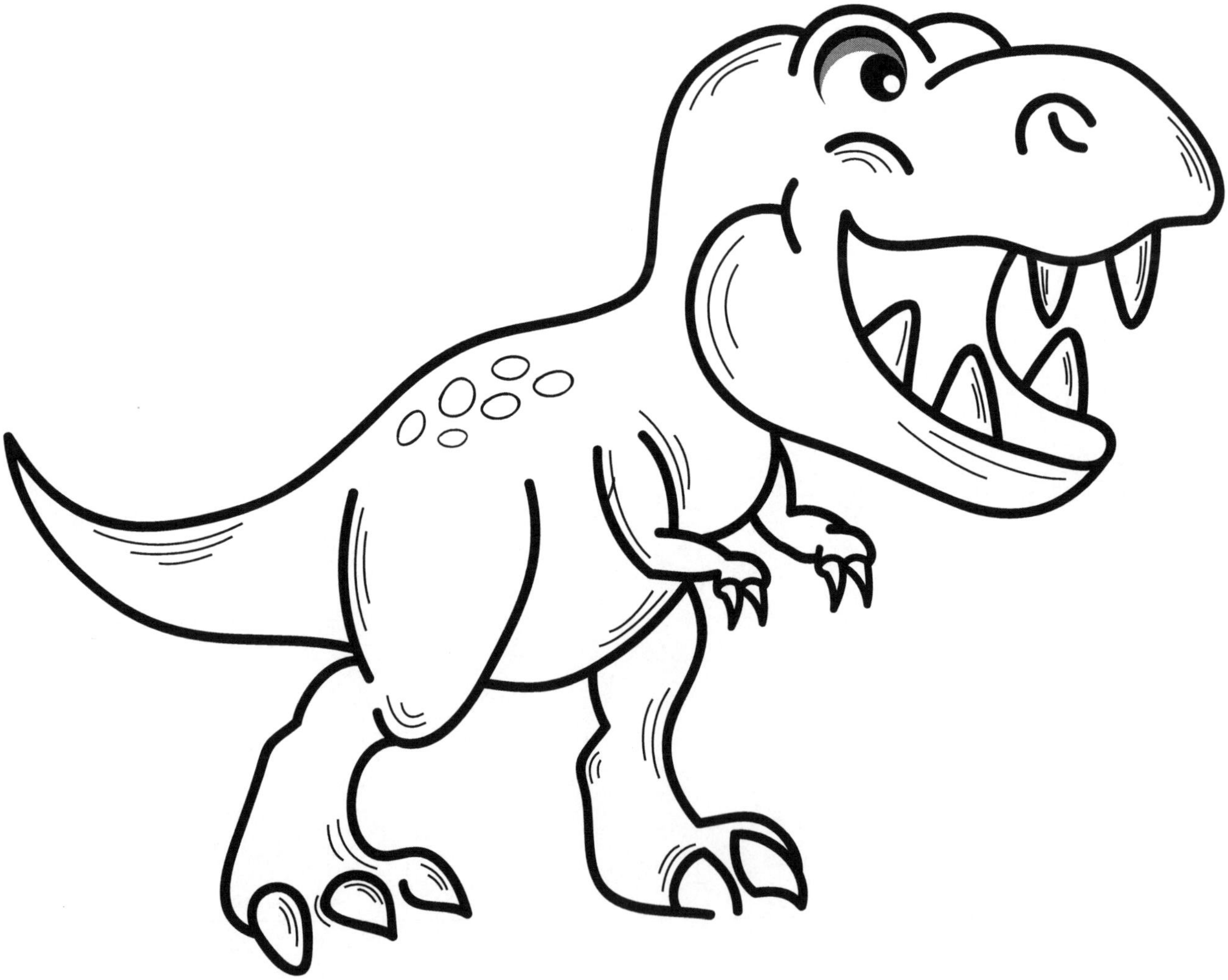

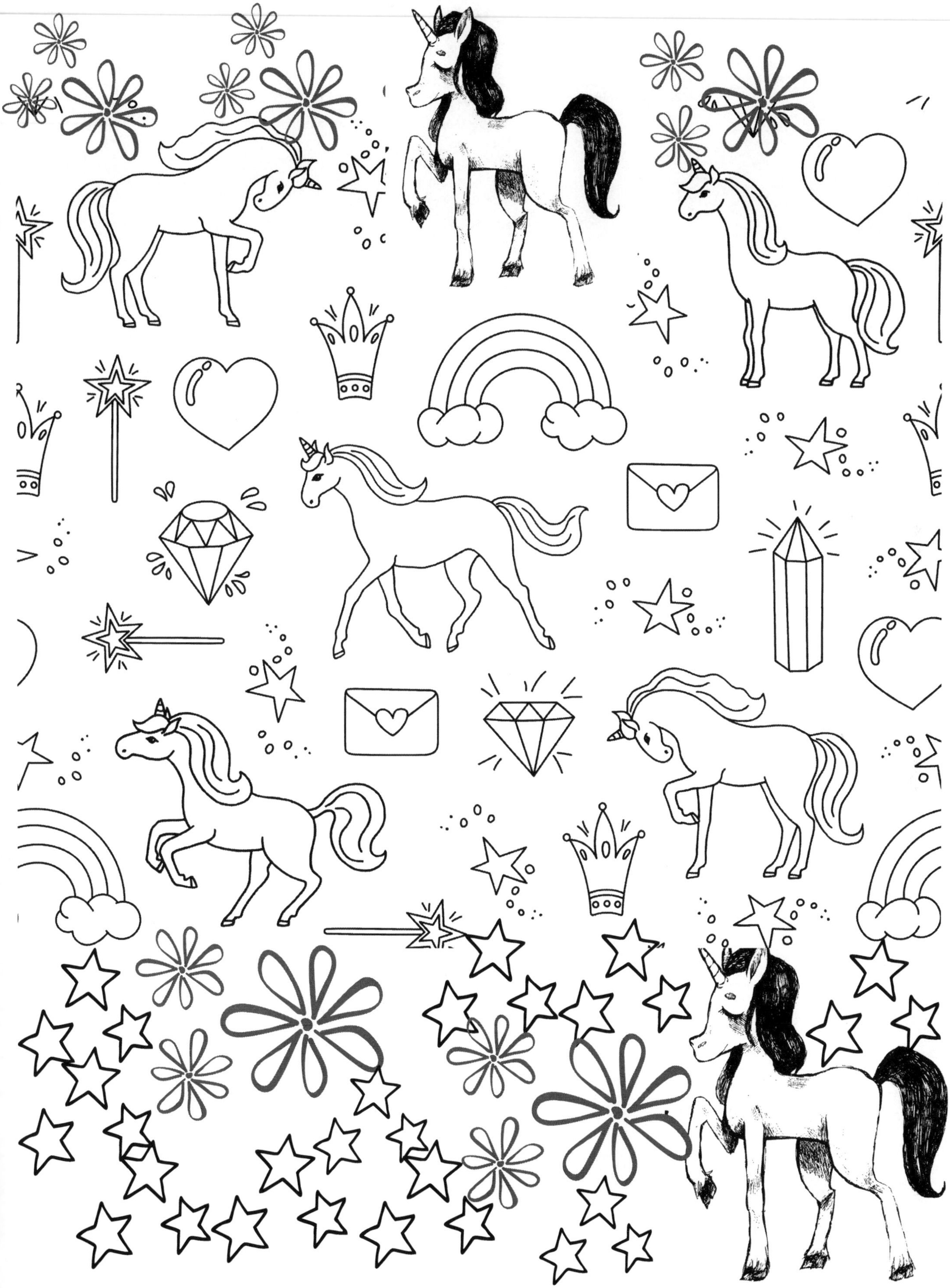

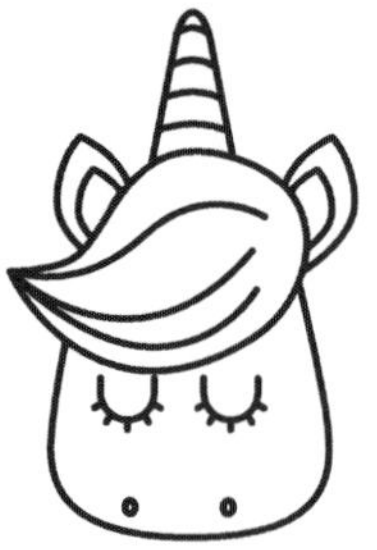

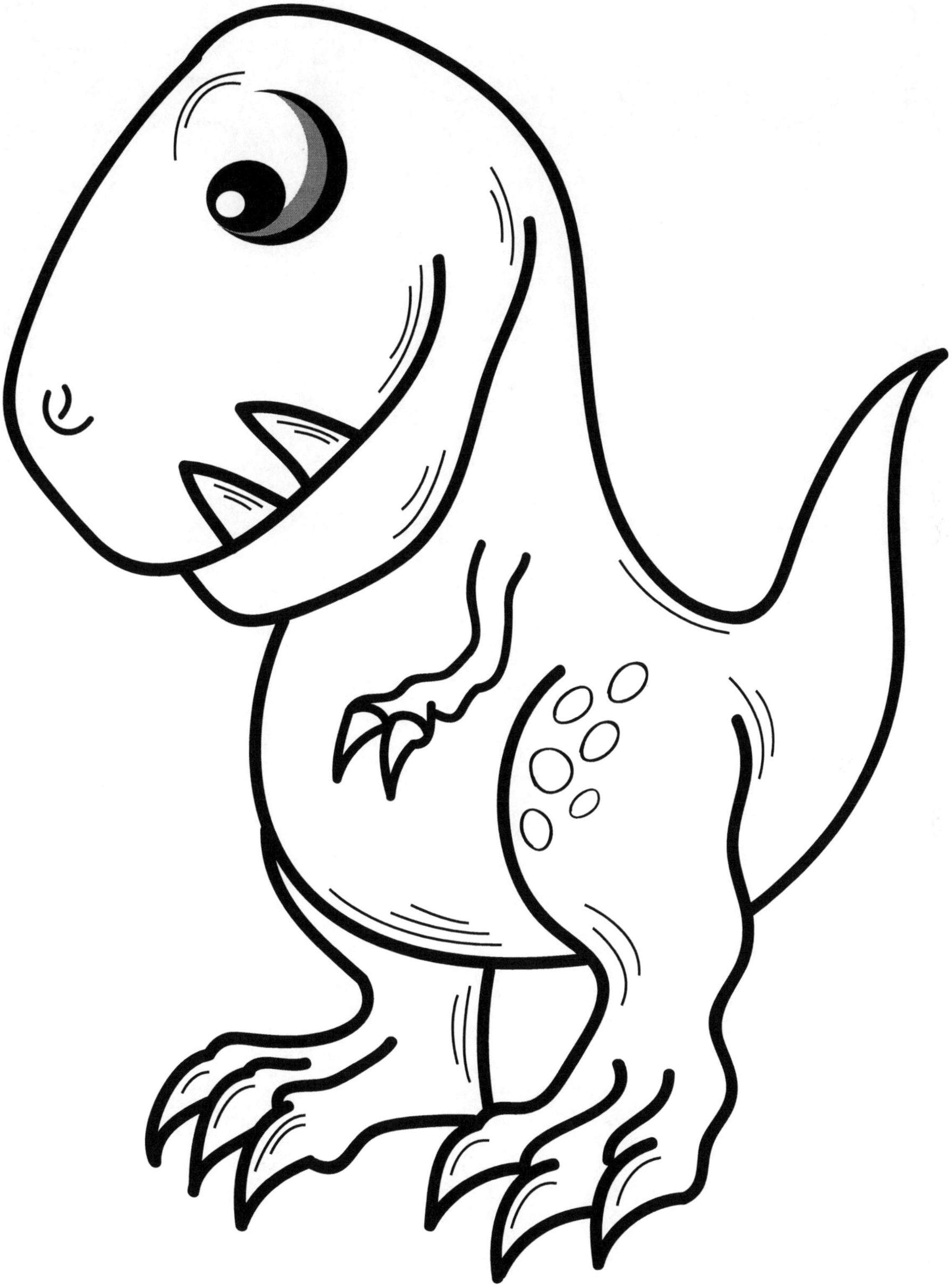

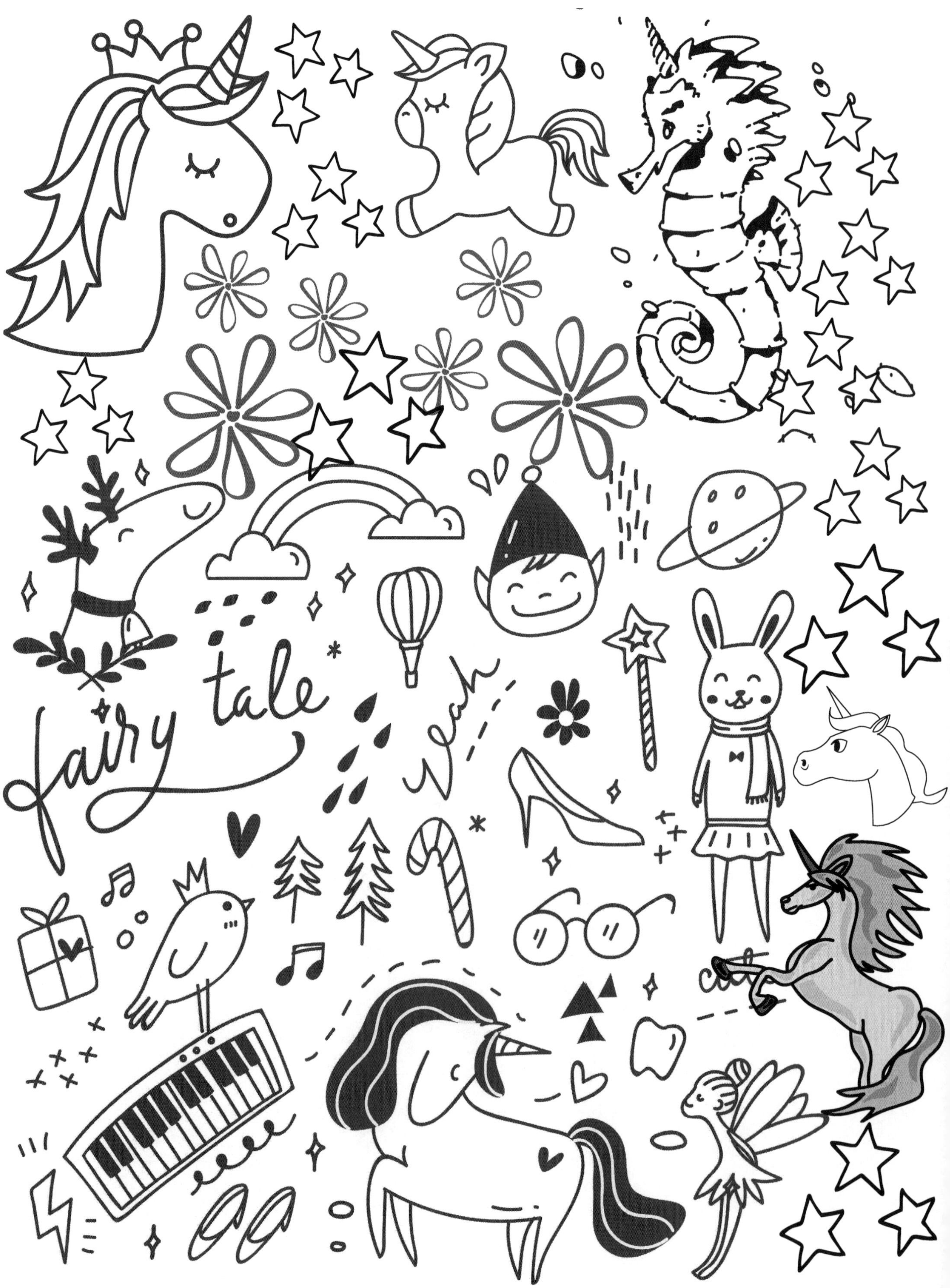
fairy tale
yeah

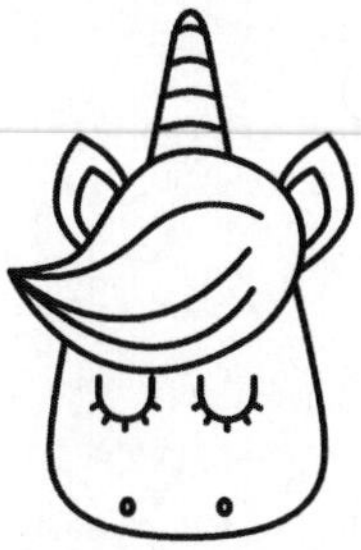

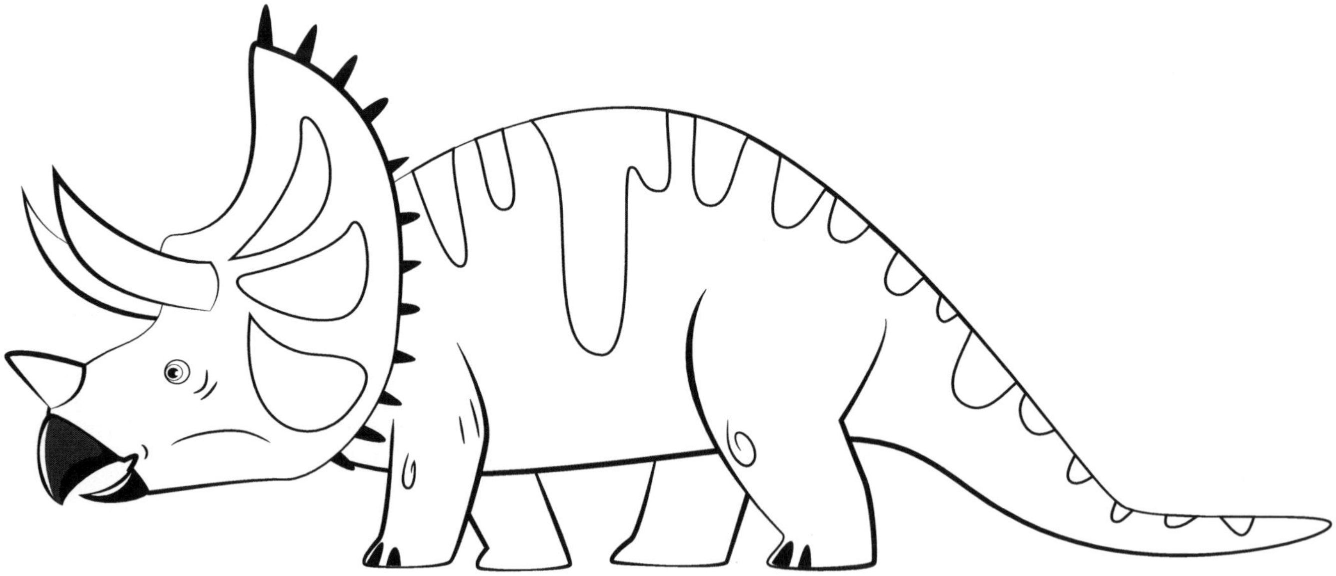

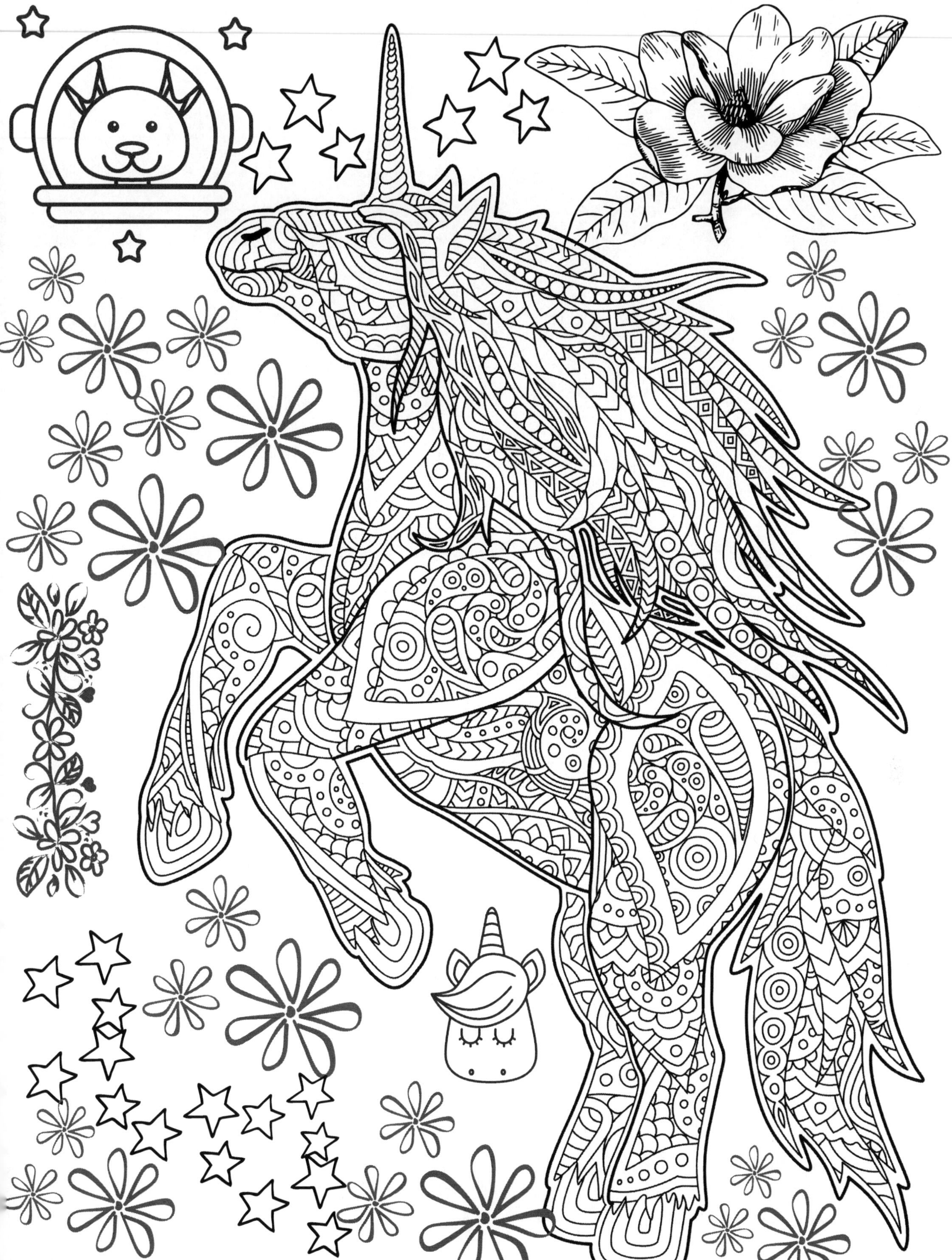

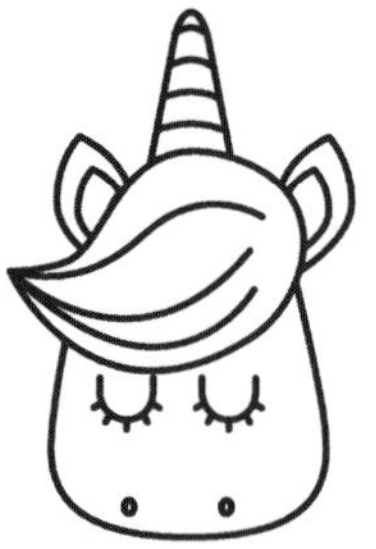

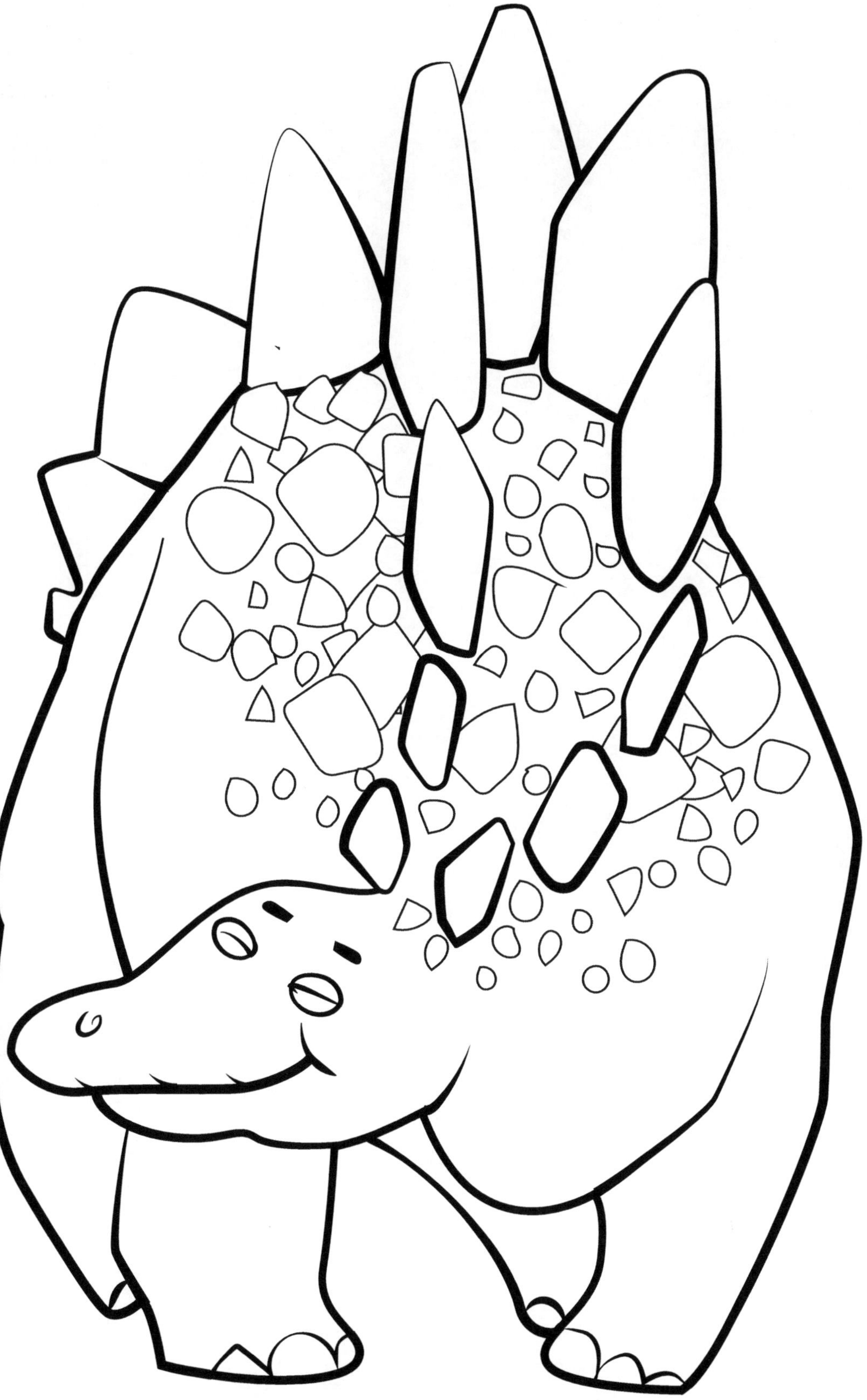

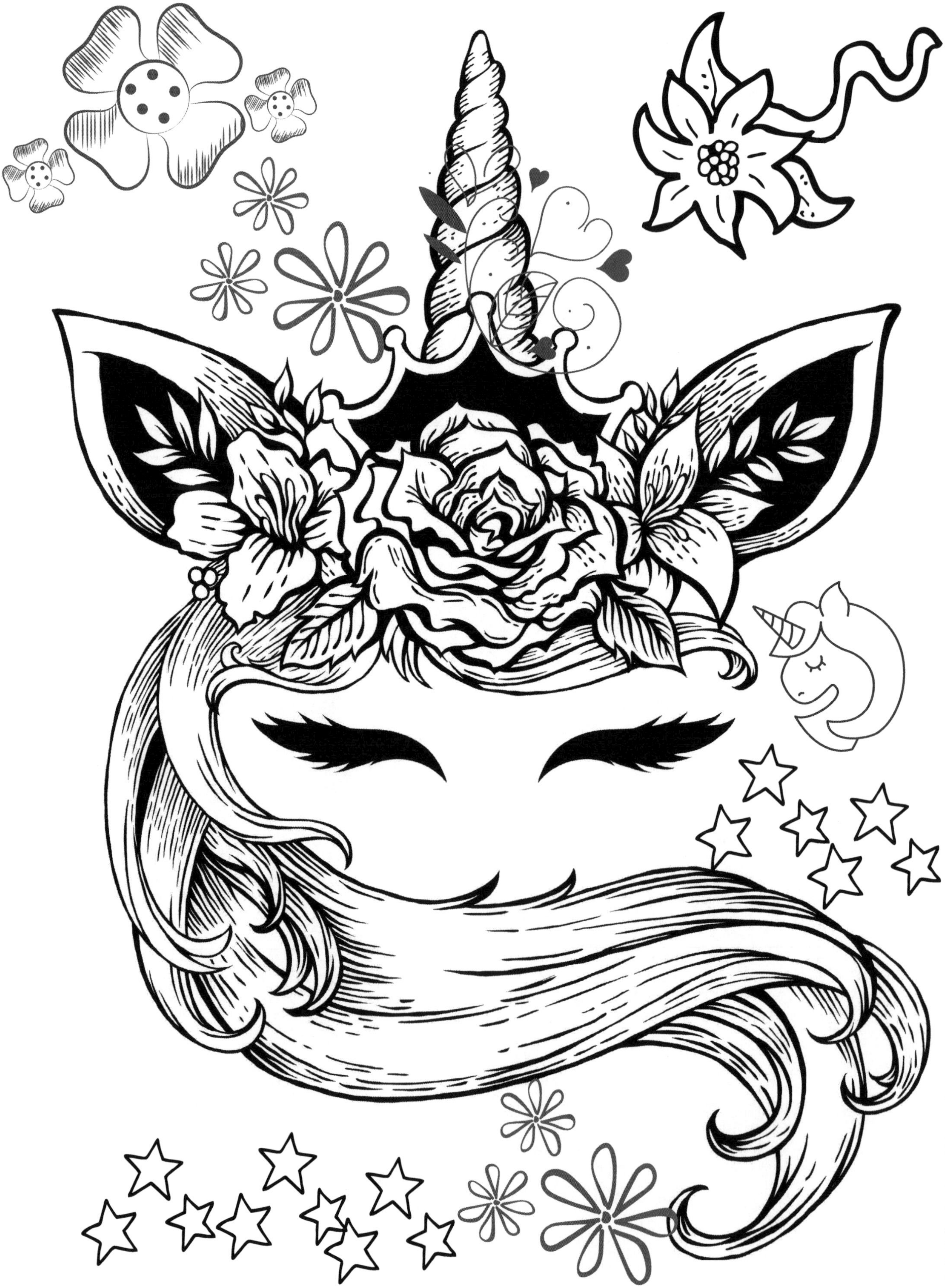

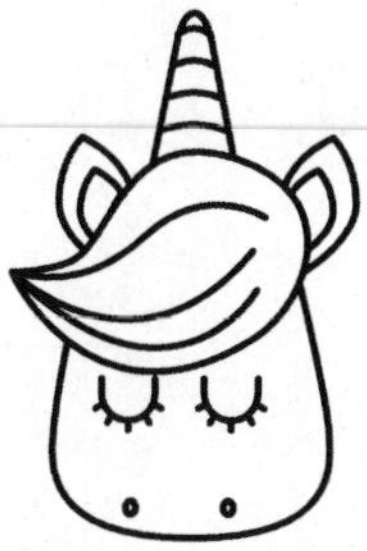

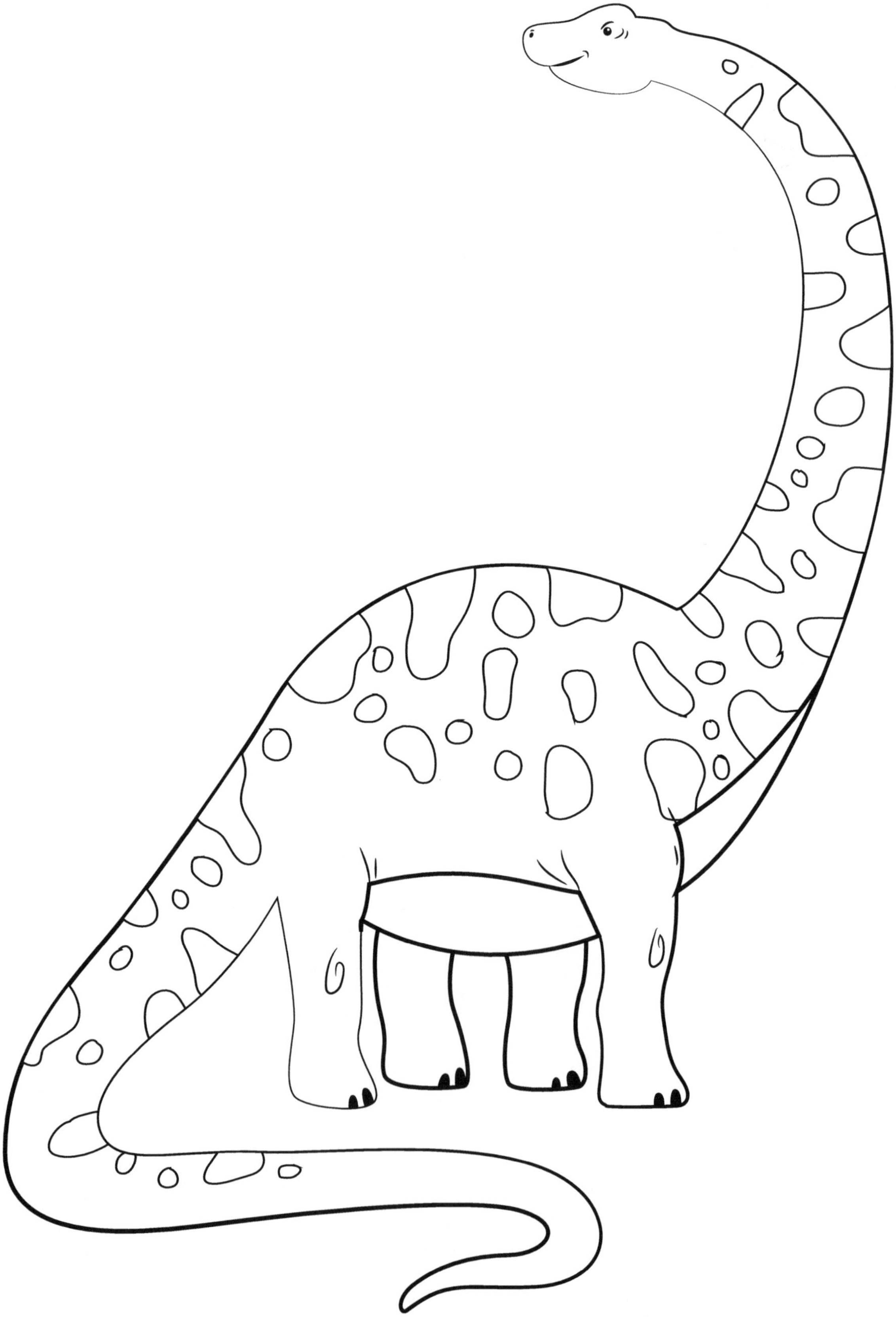

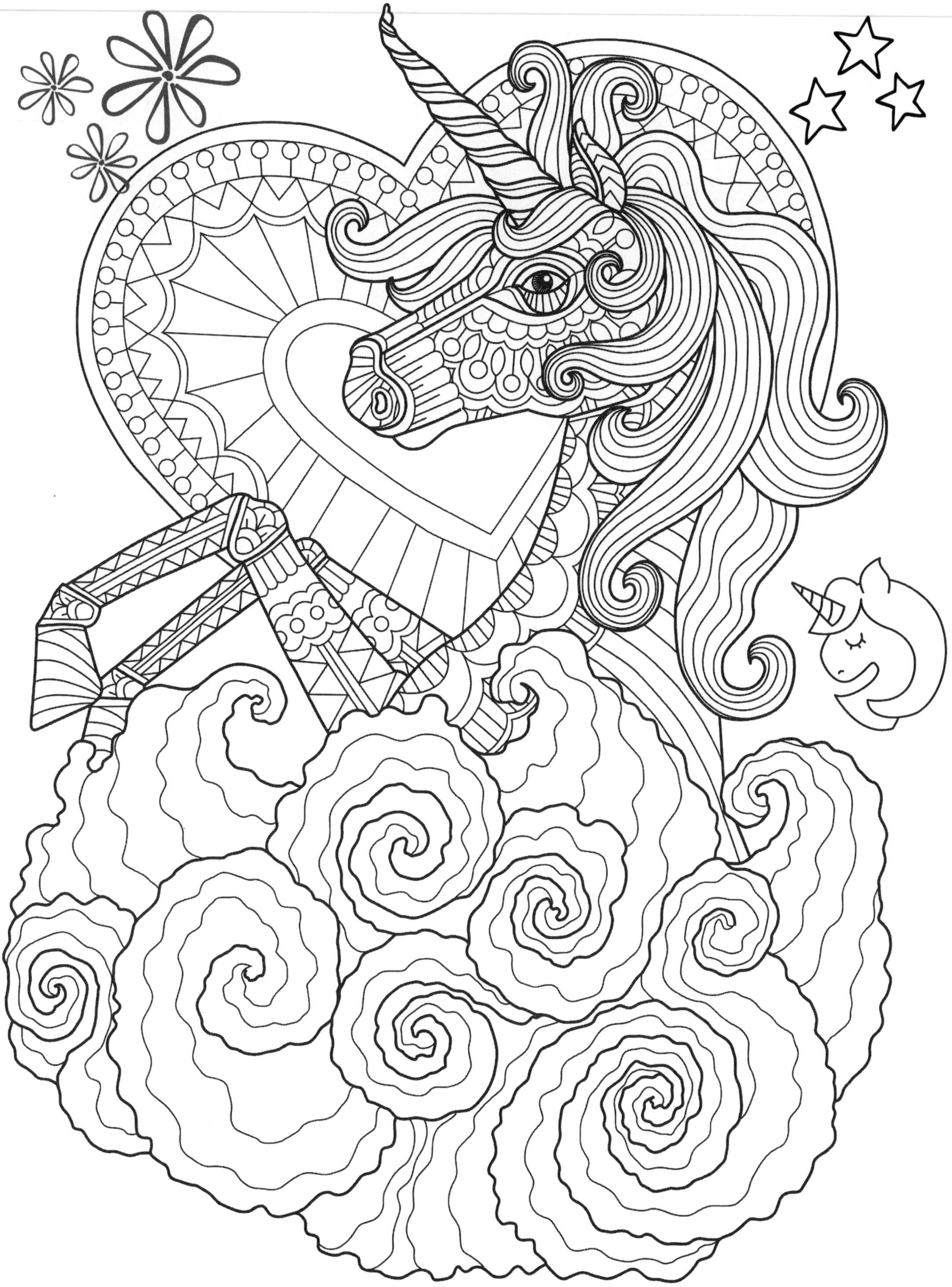

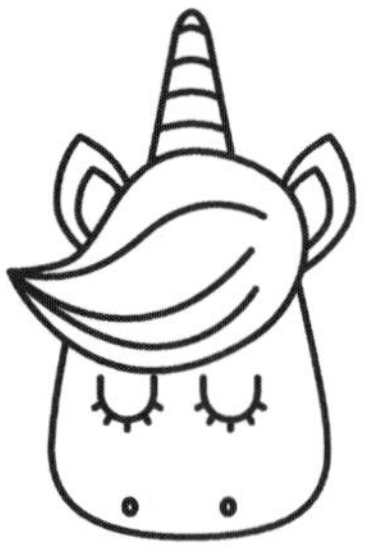

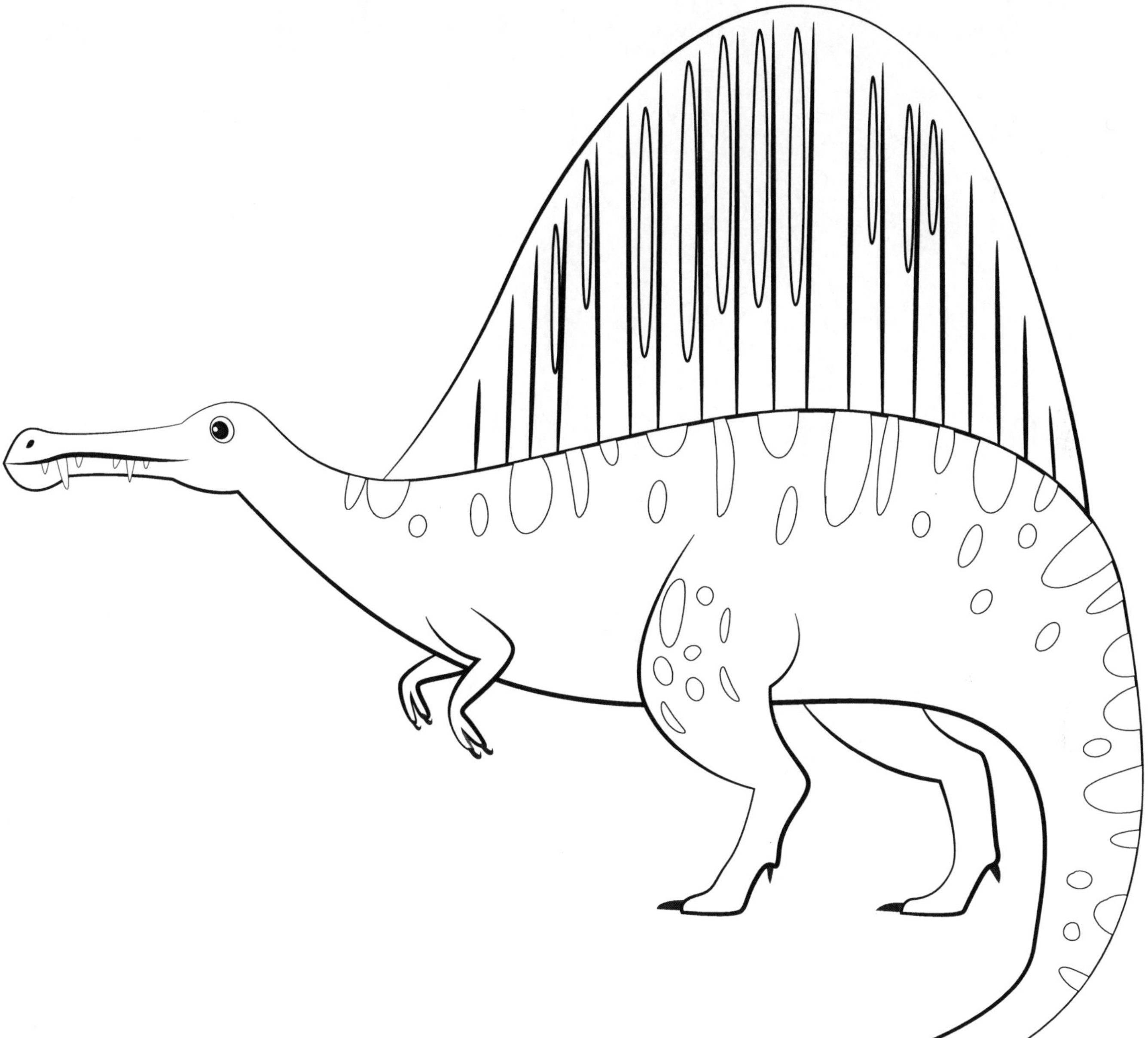

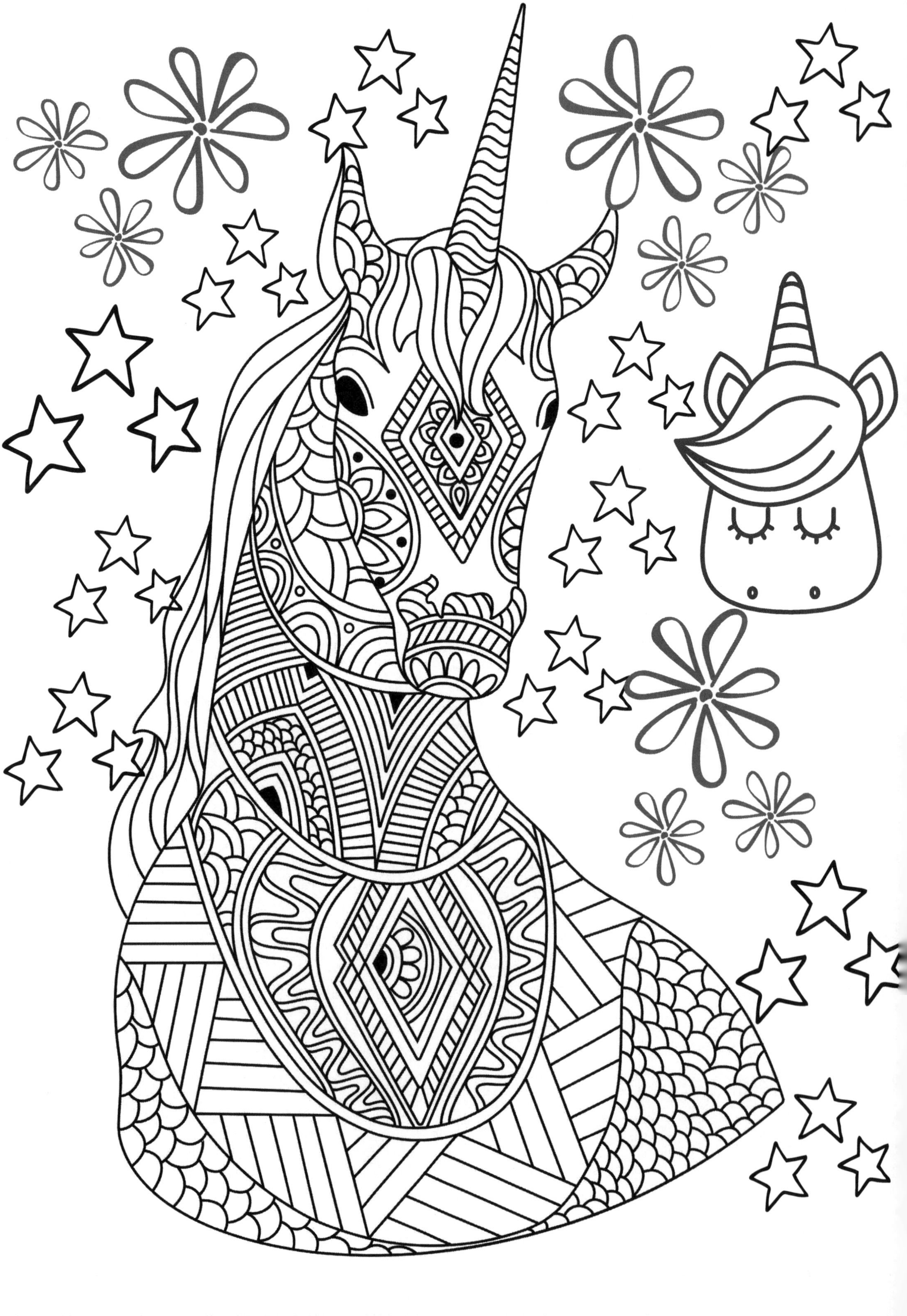

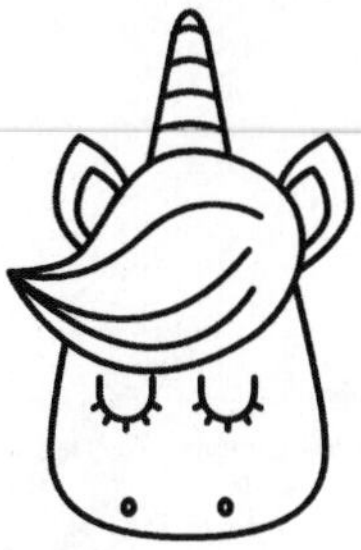

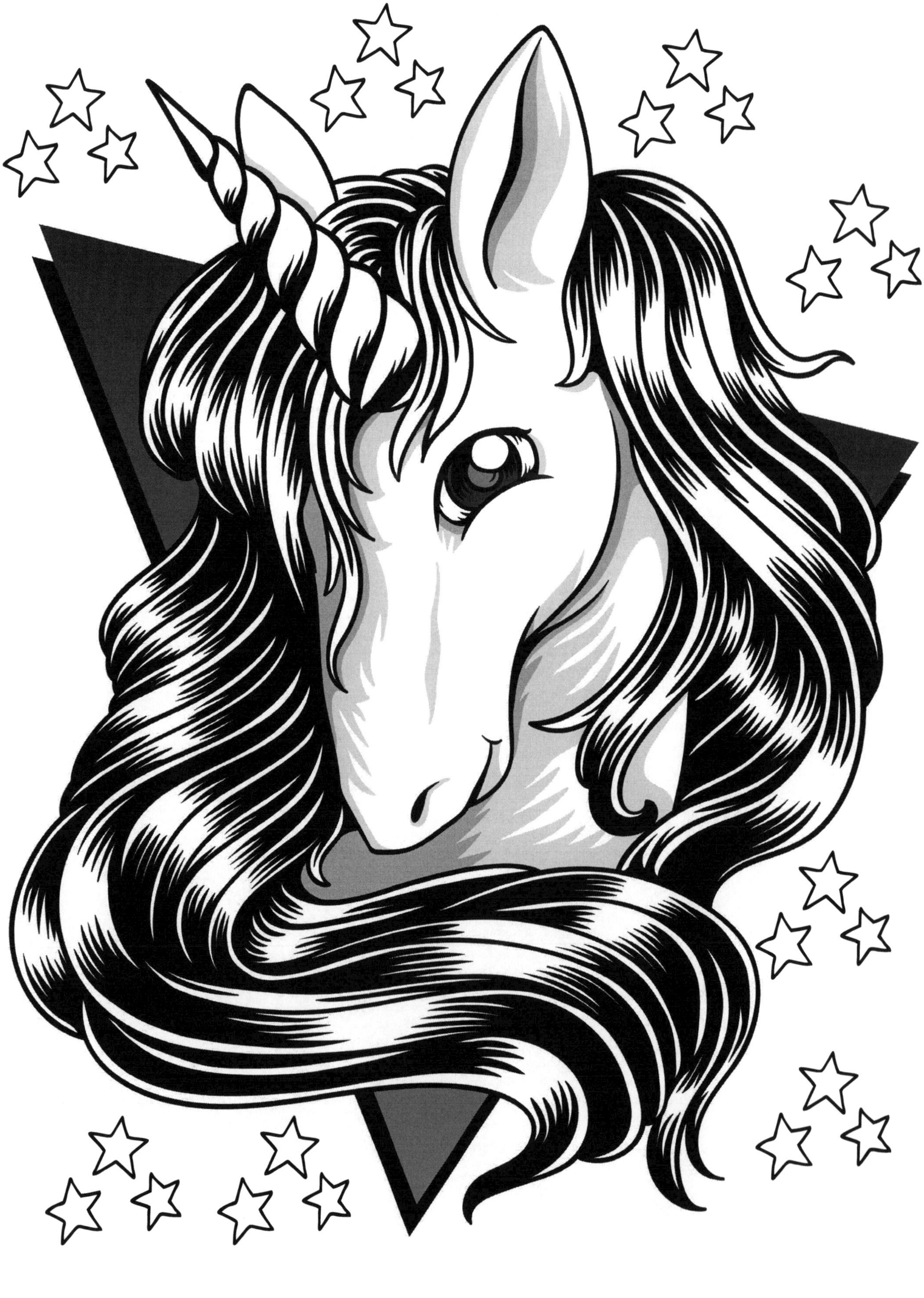

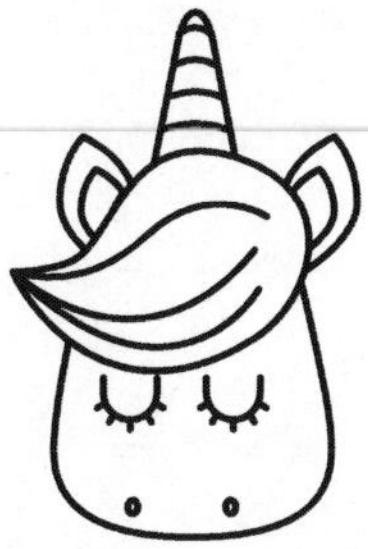

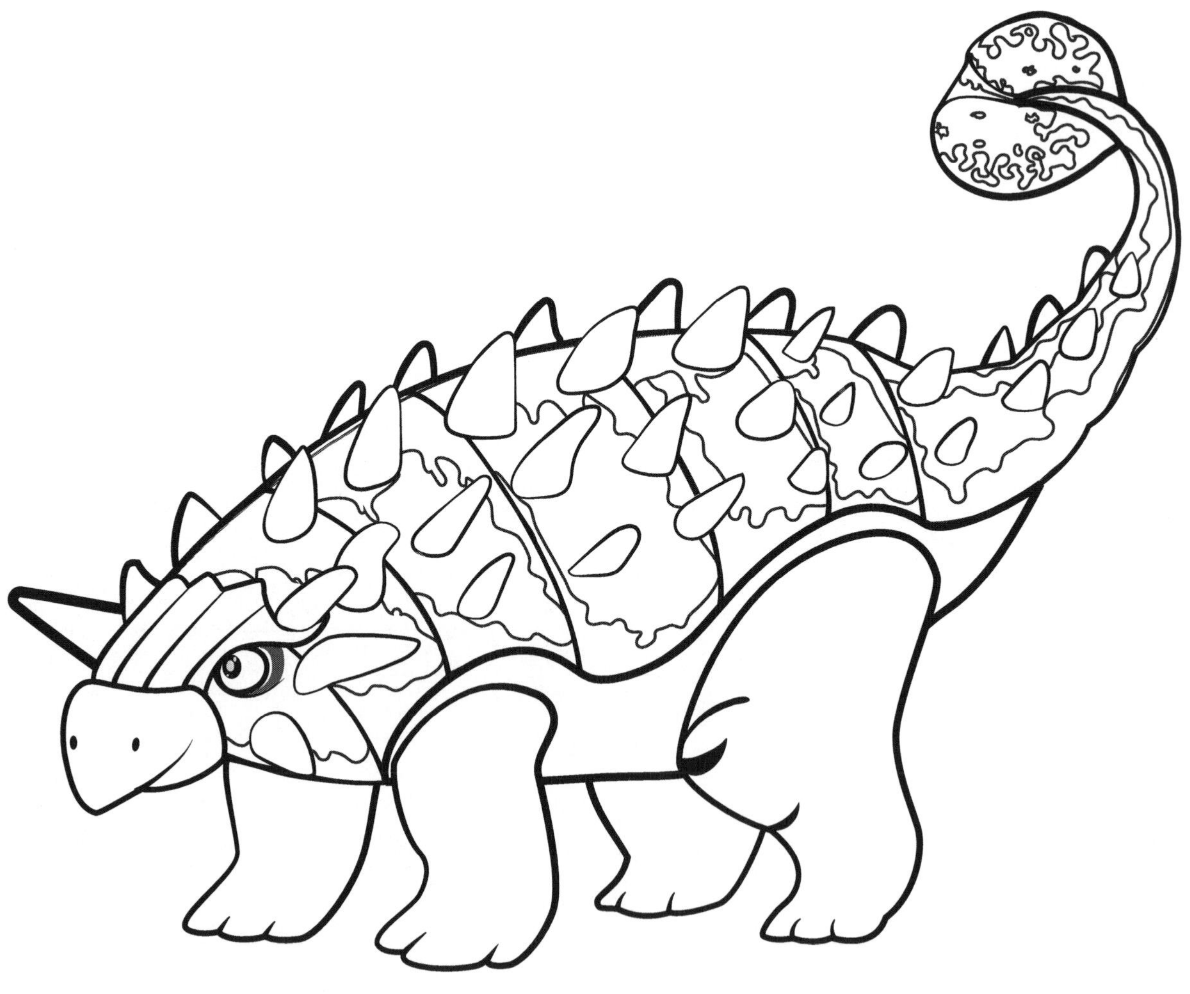

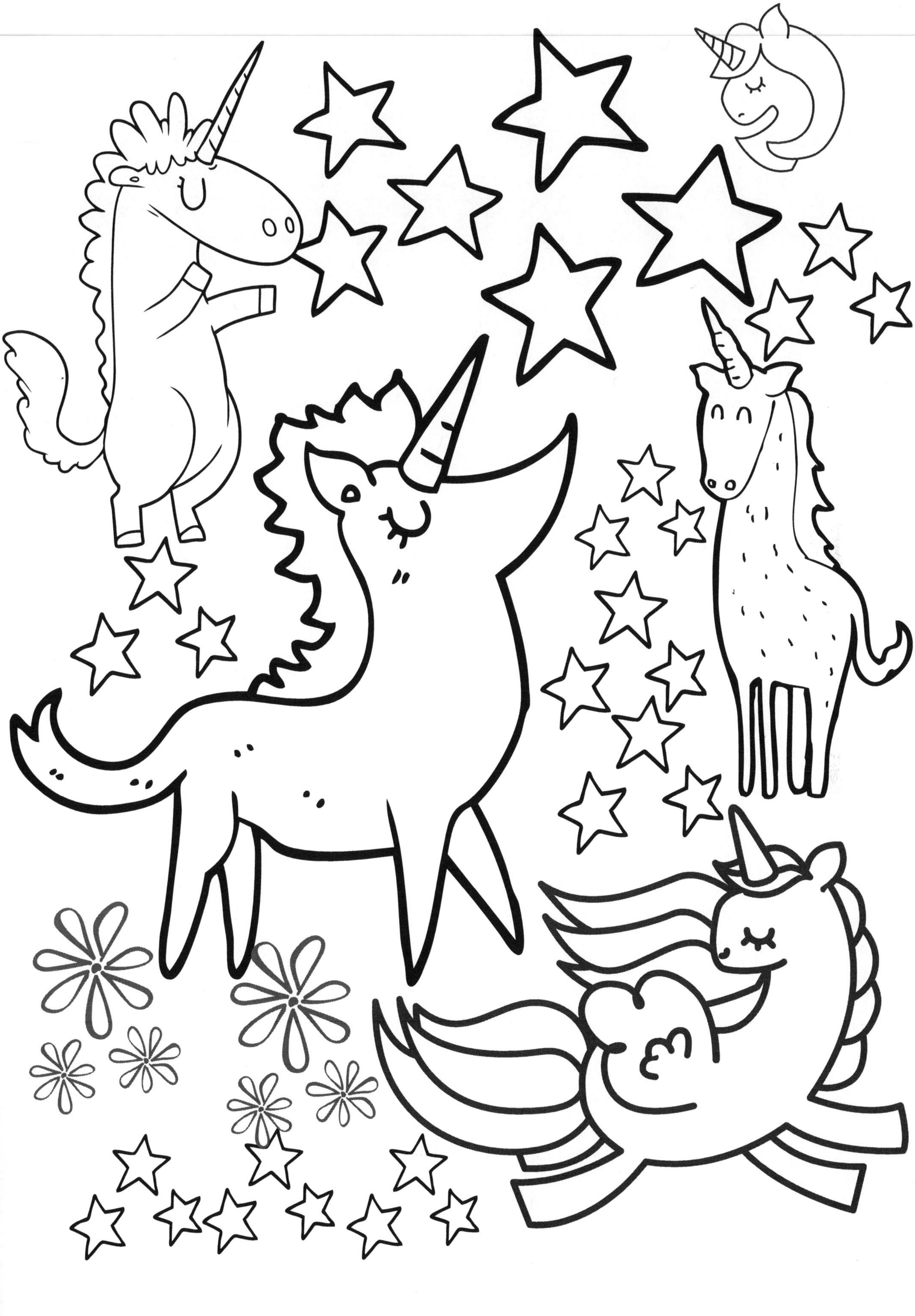

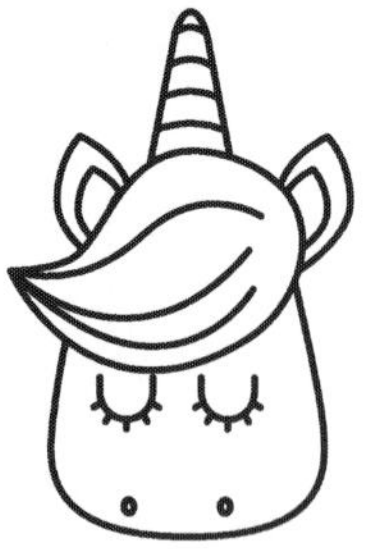

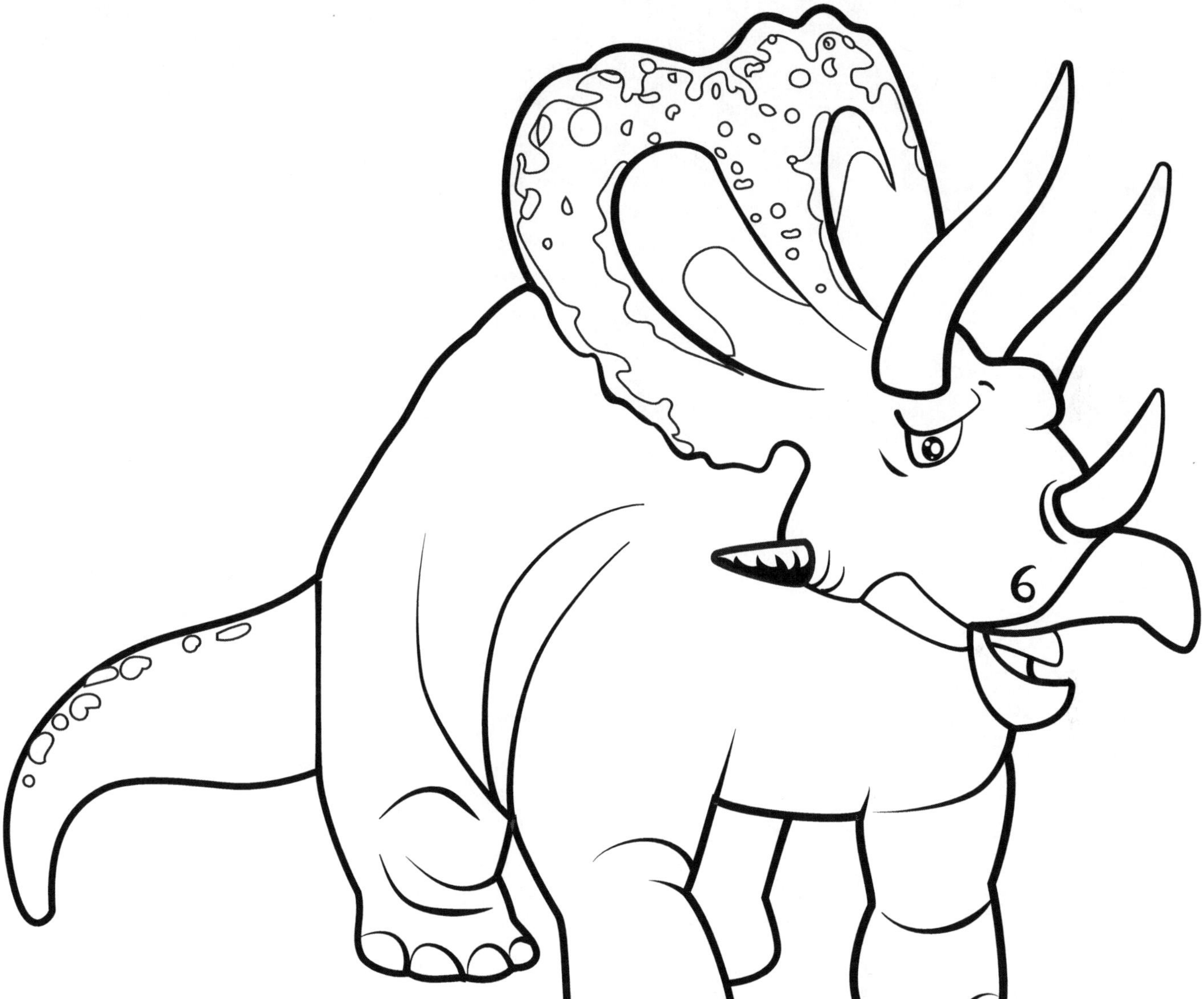

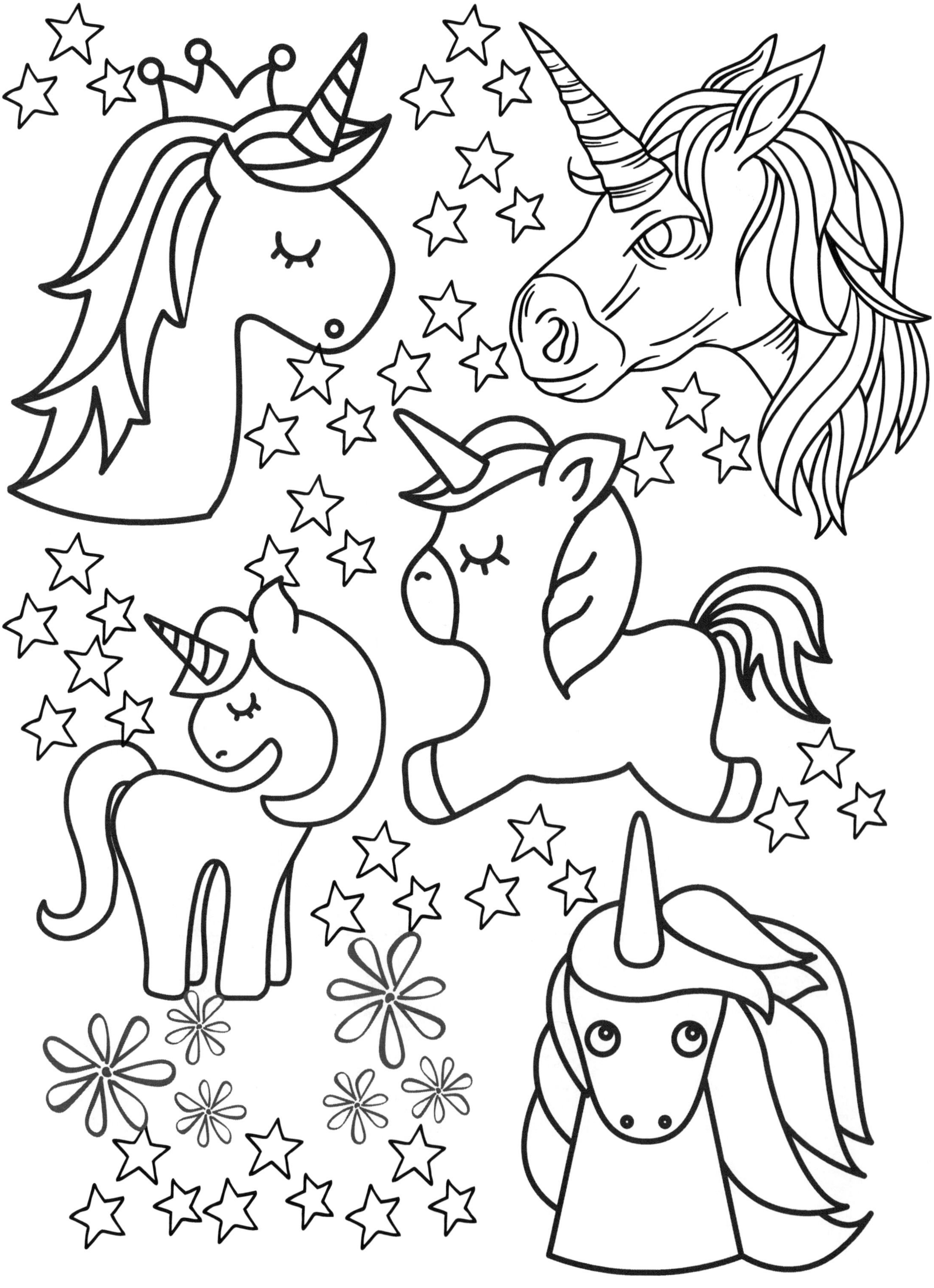

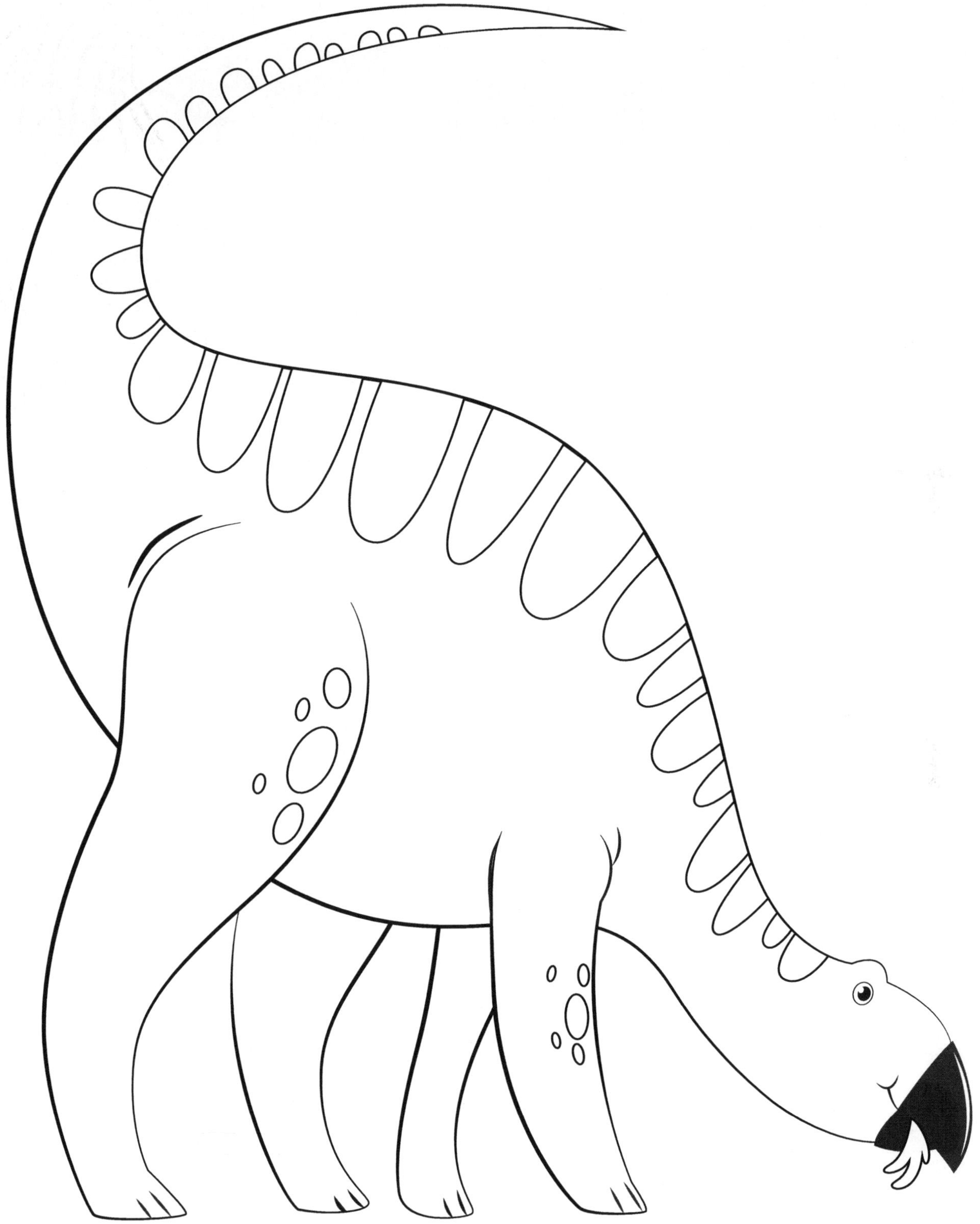

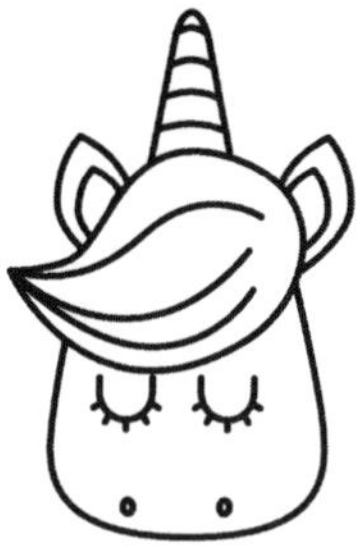

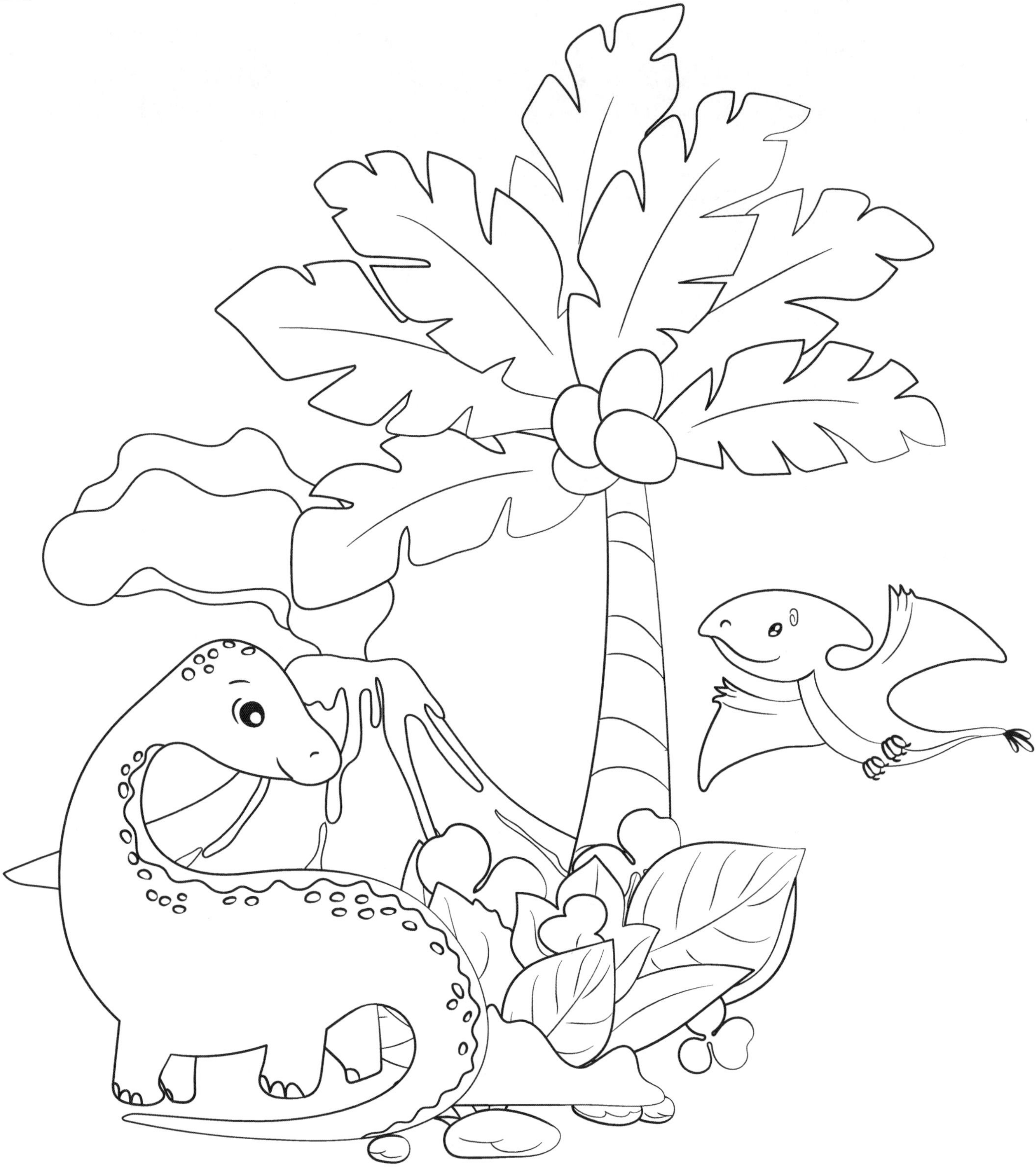

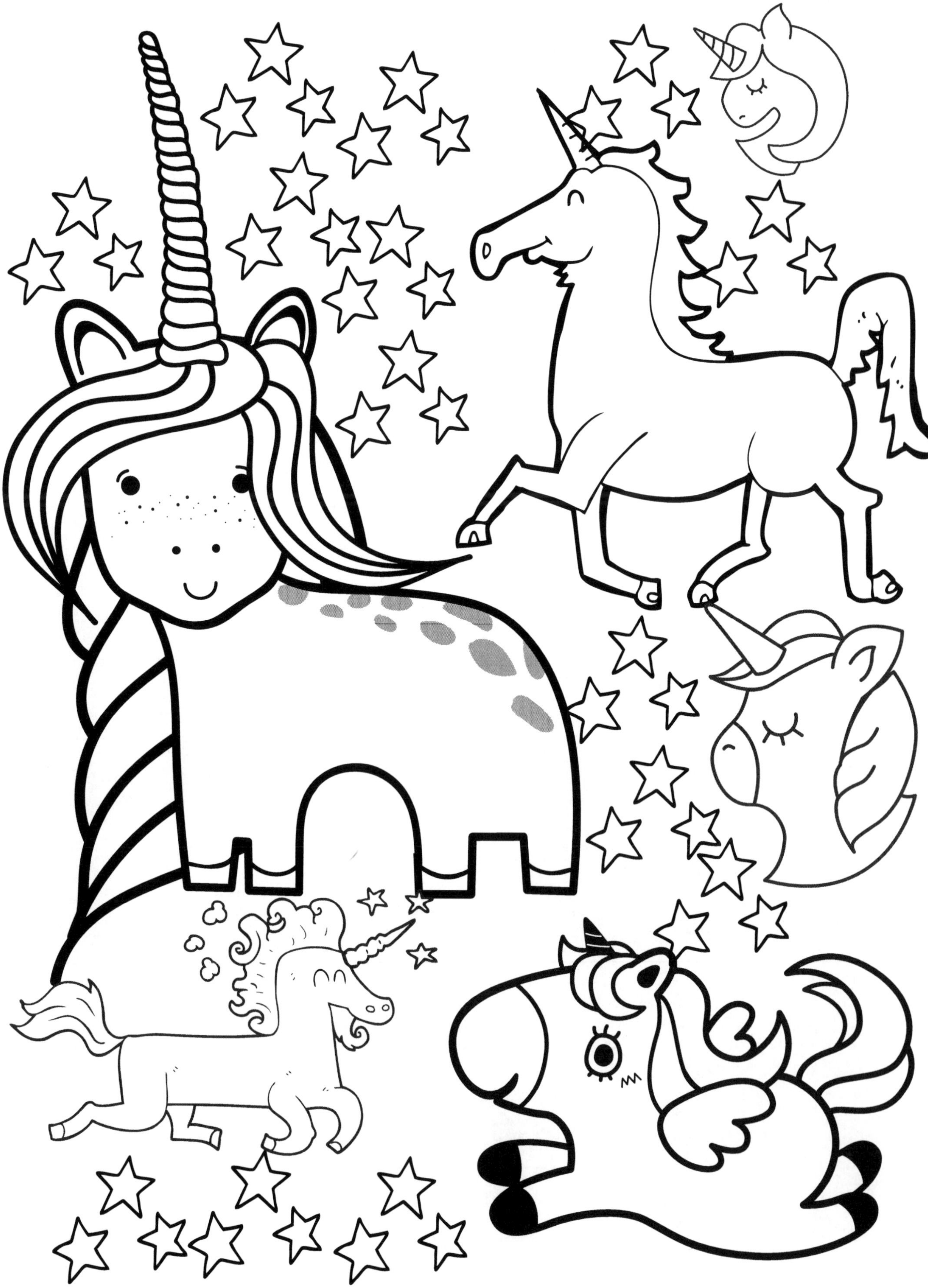

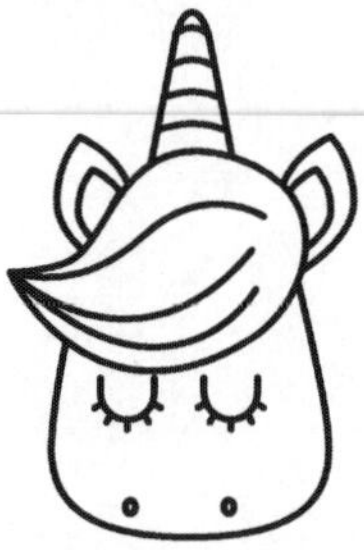

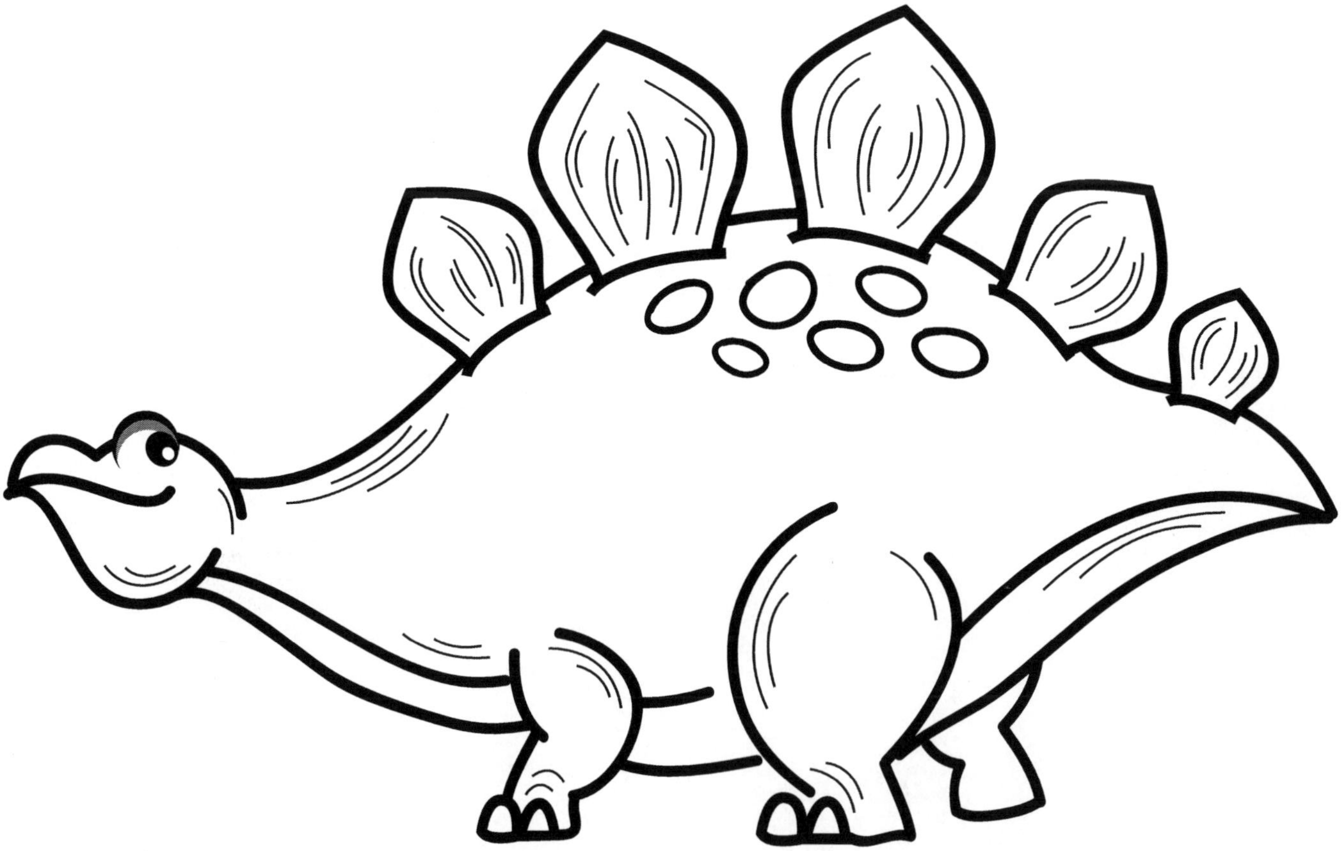

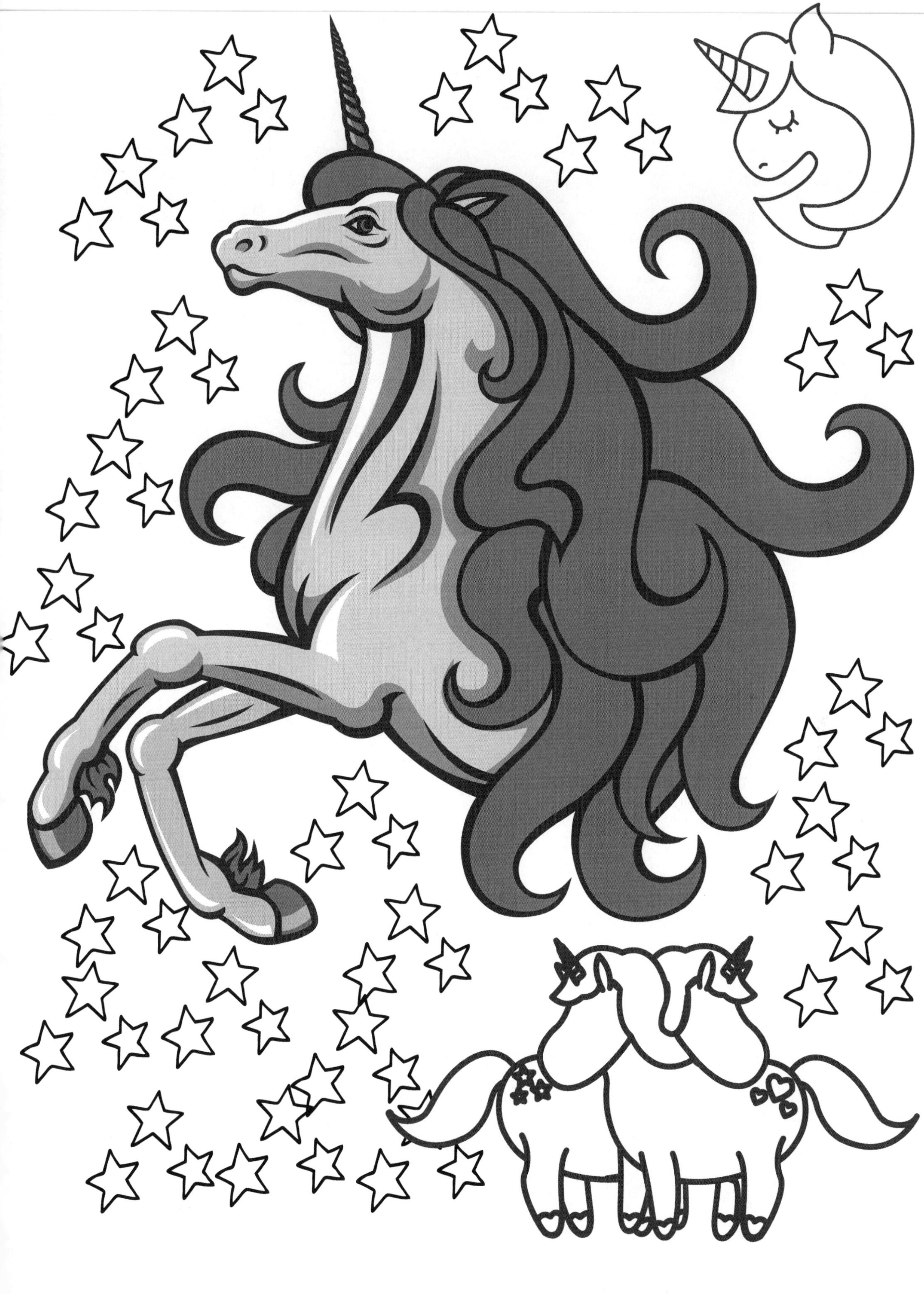

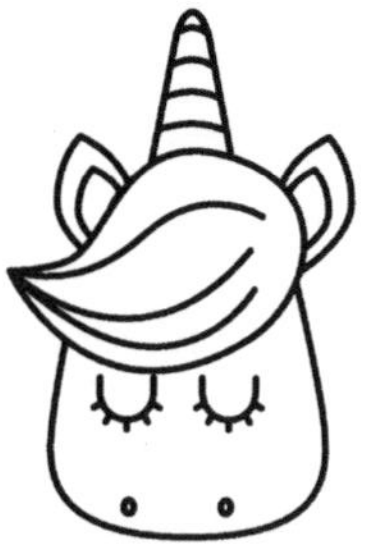

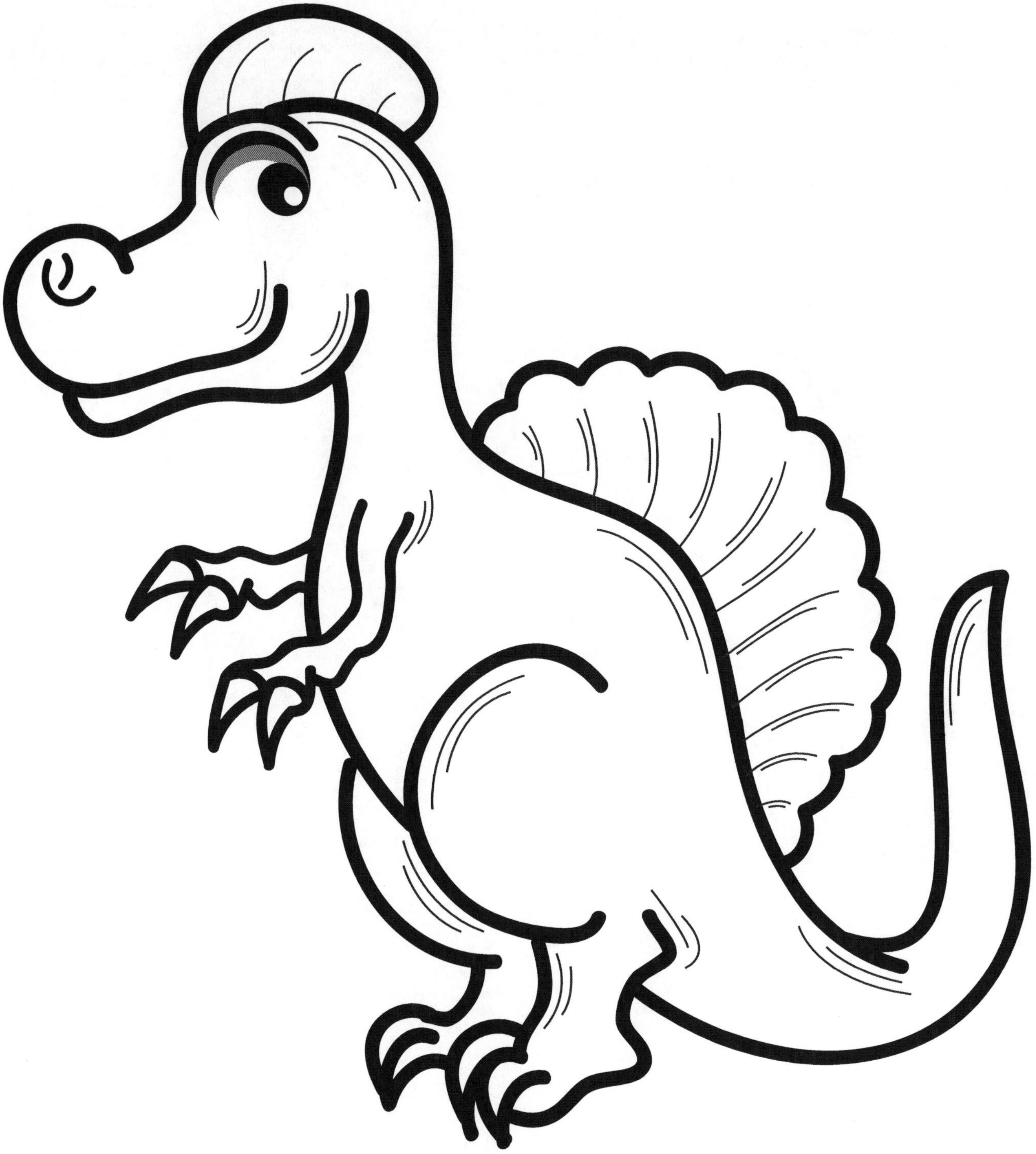

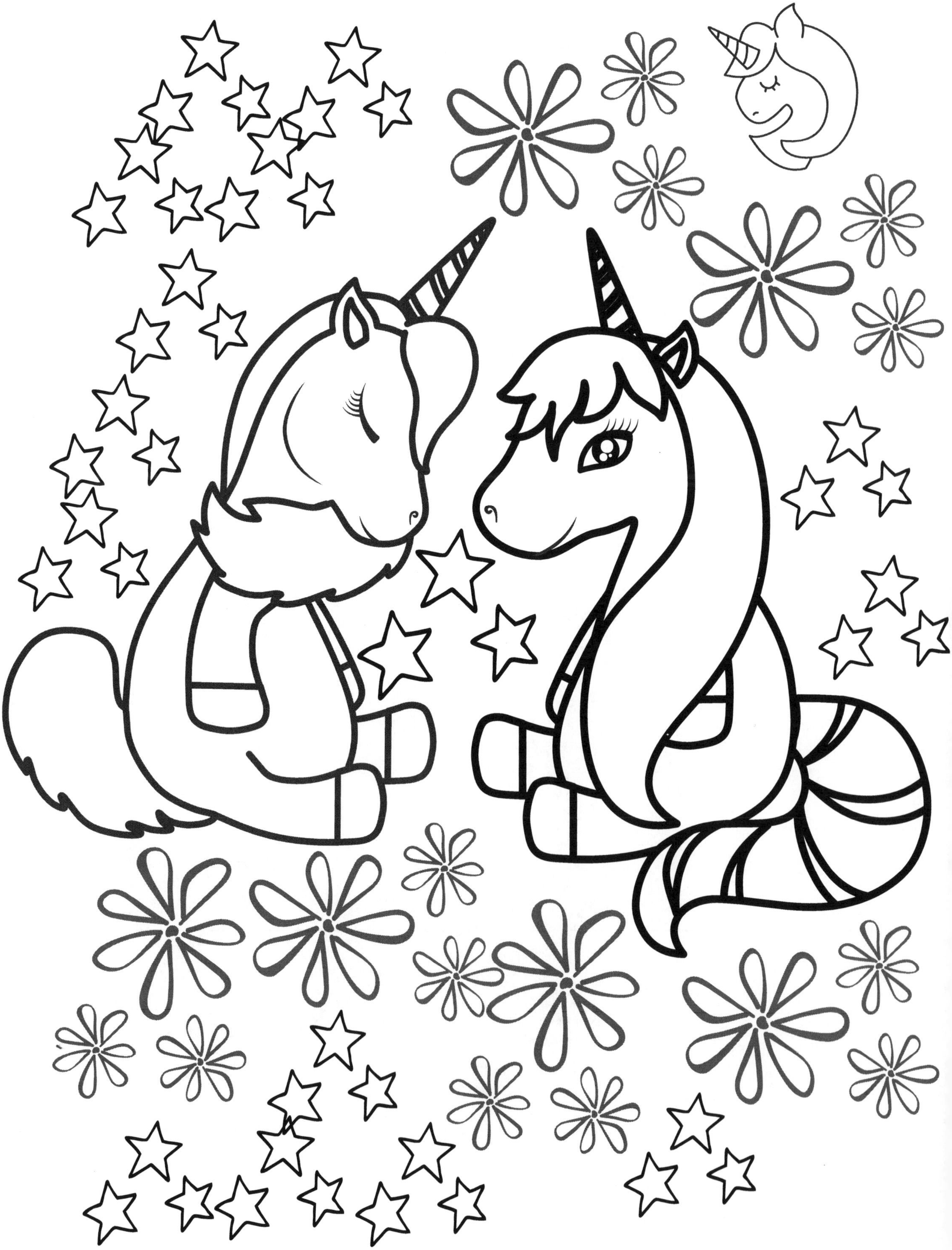

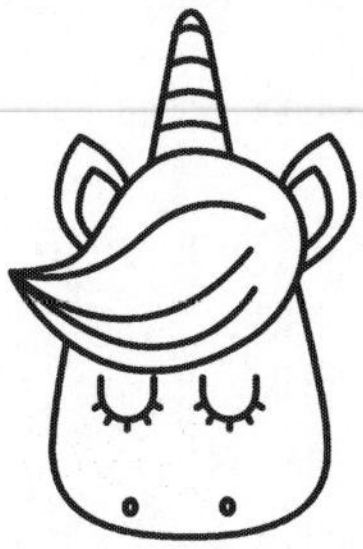

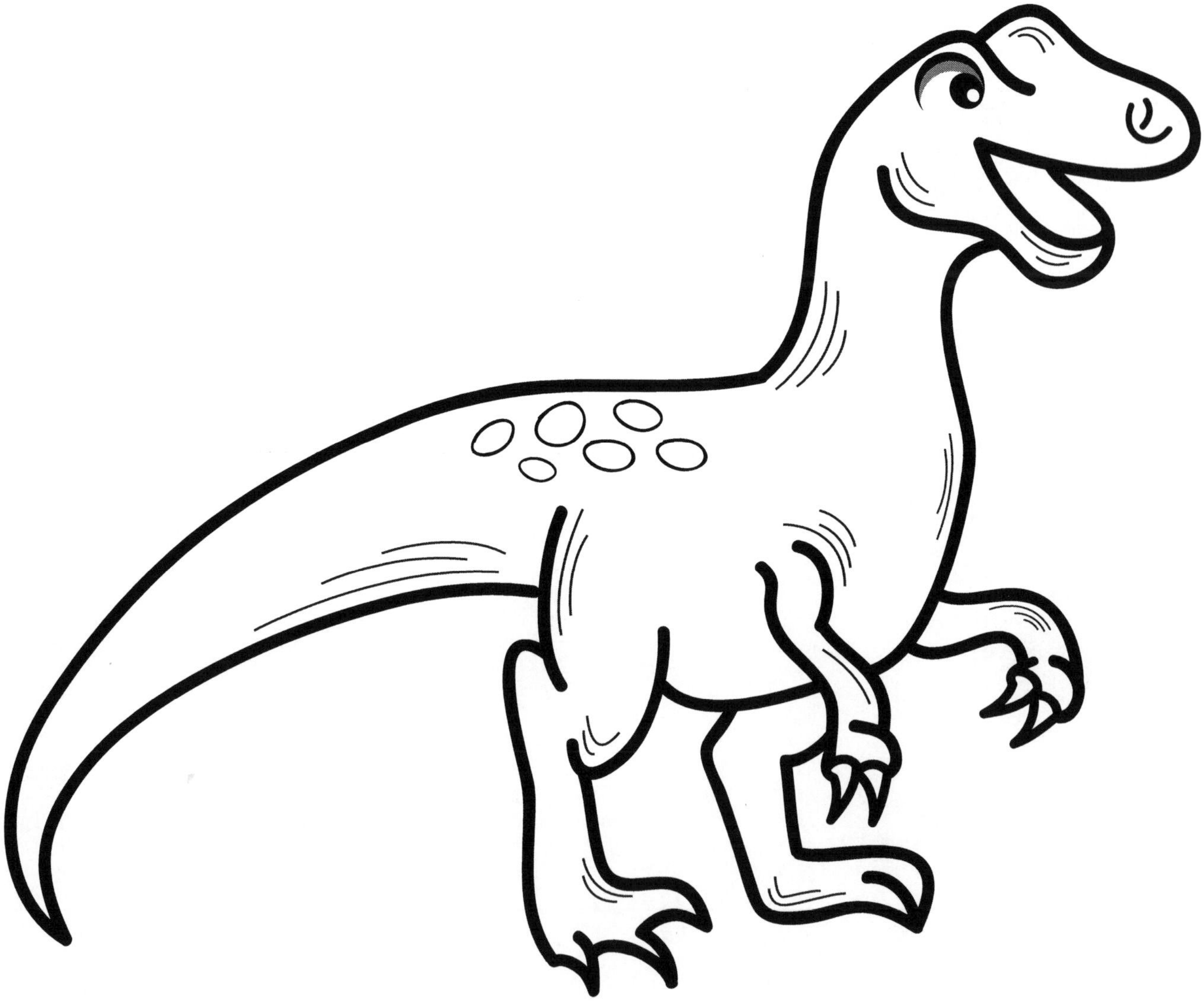

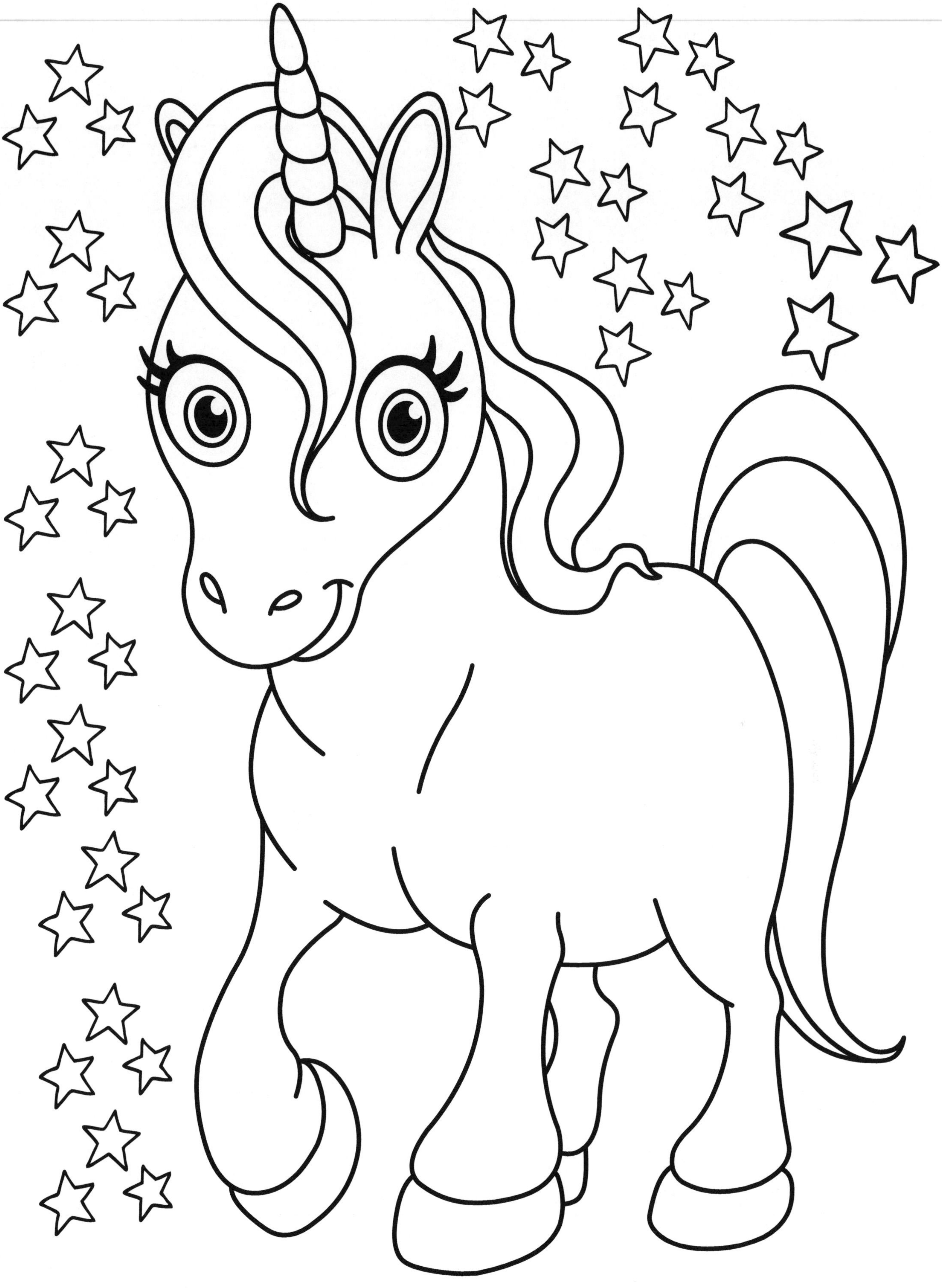

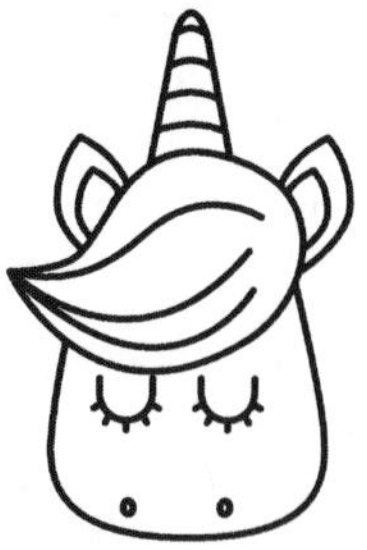

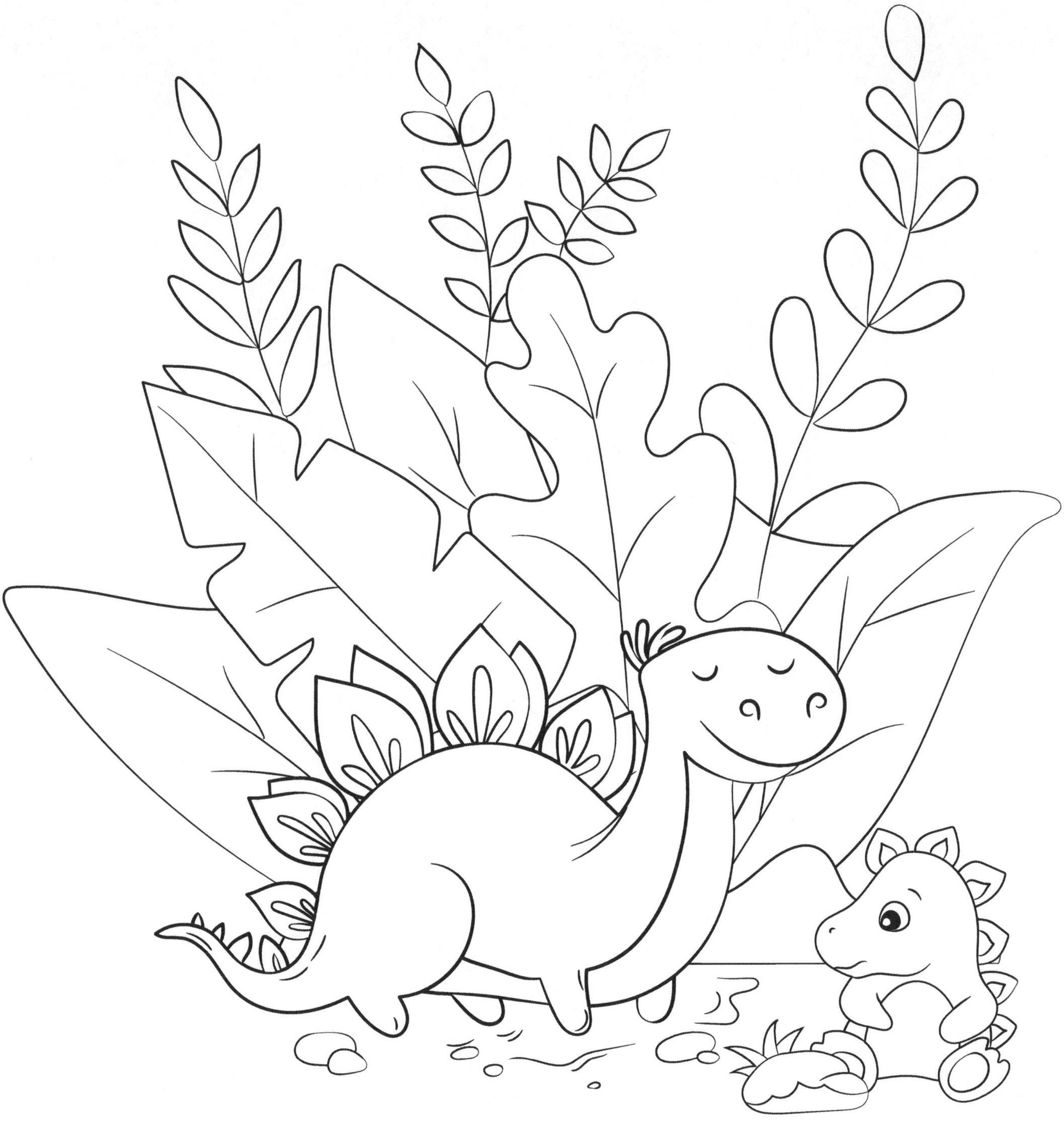

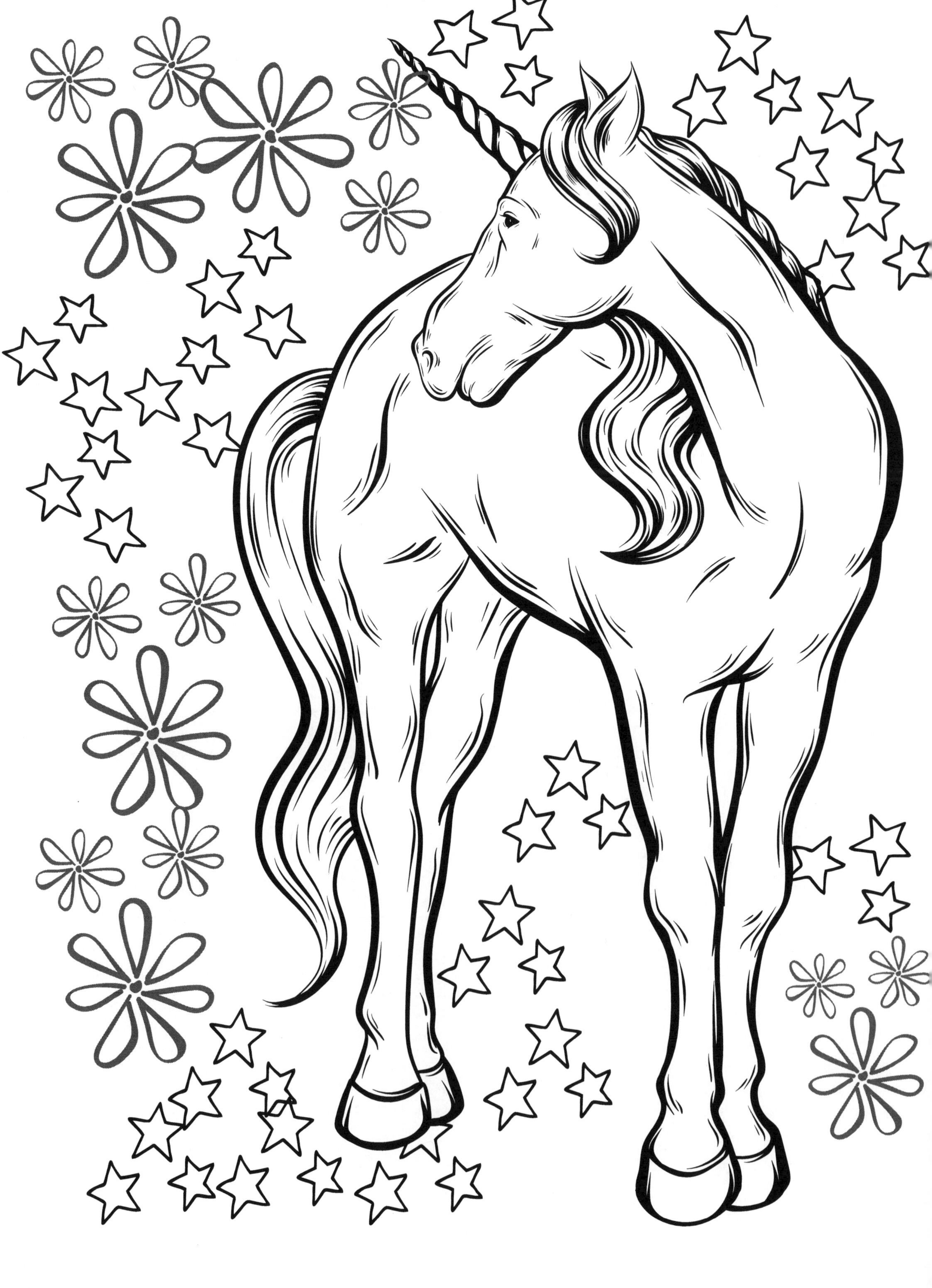

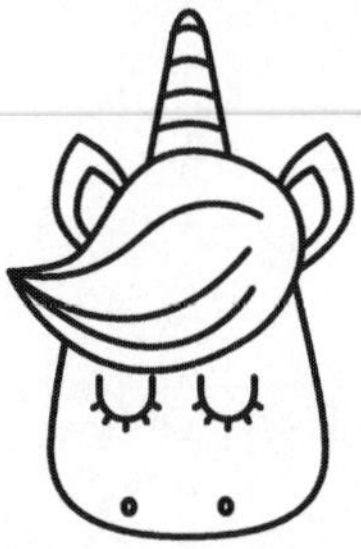

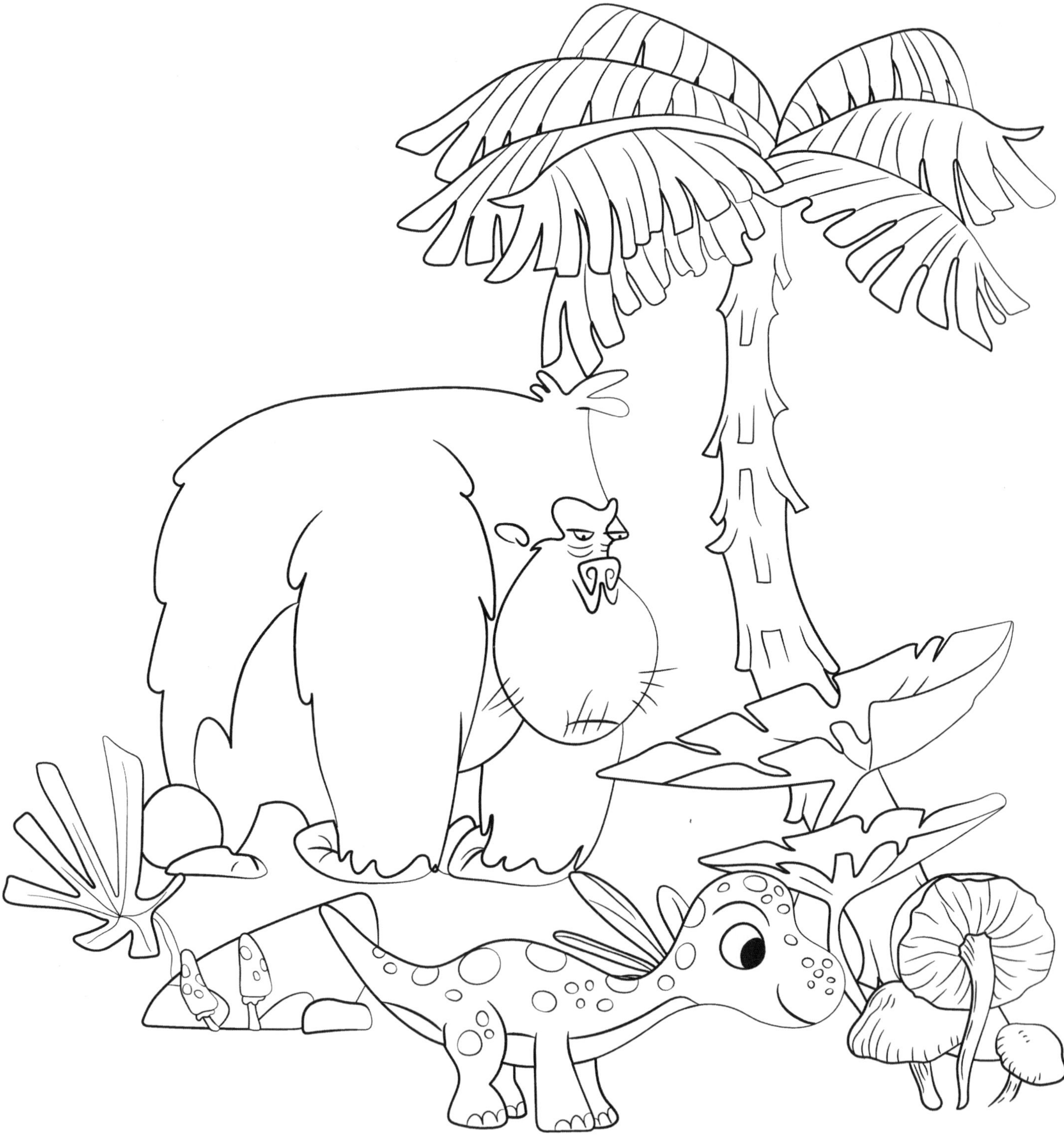

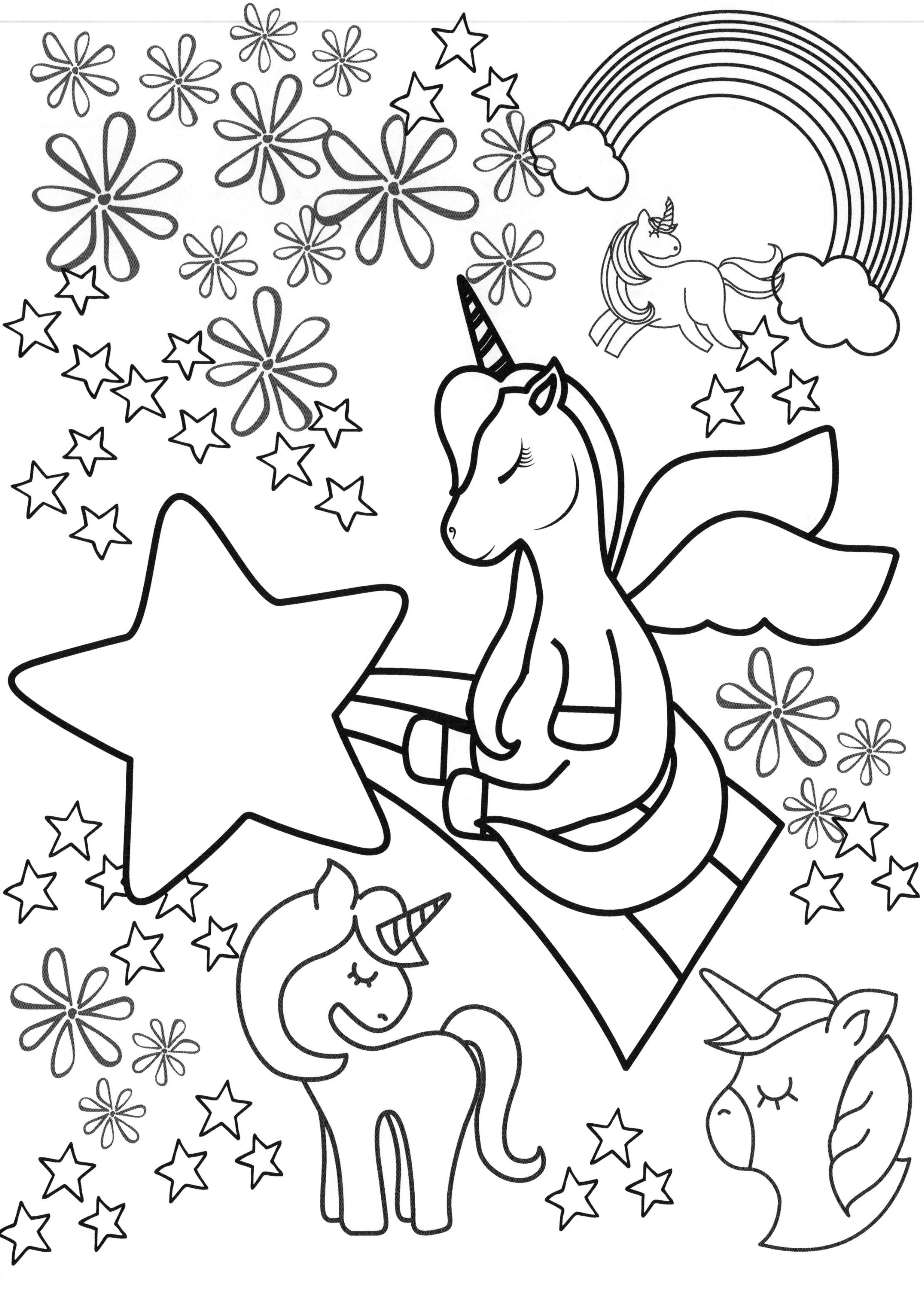

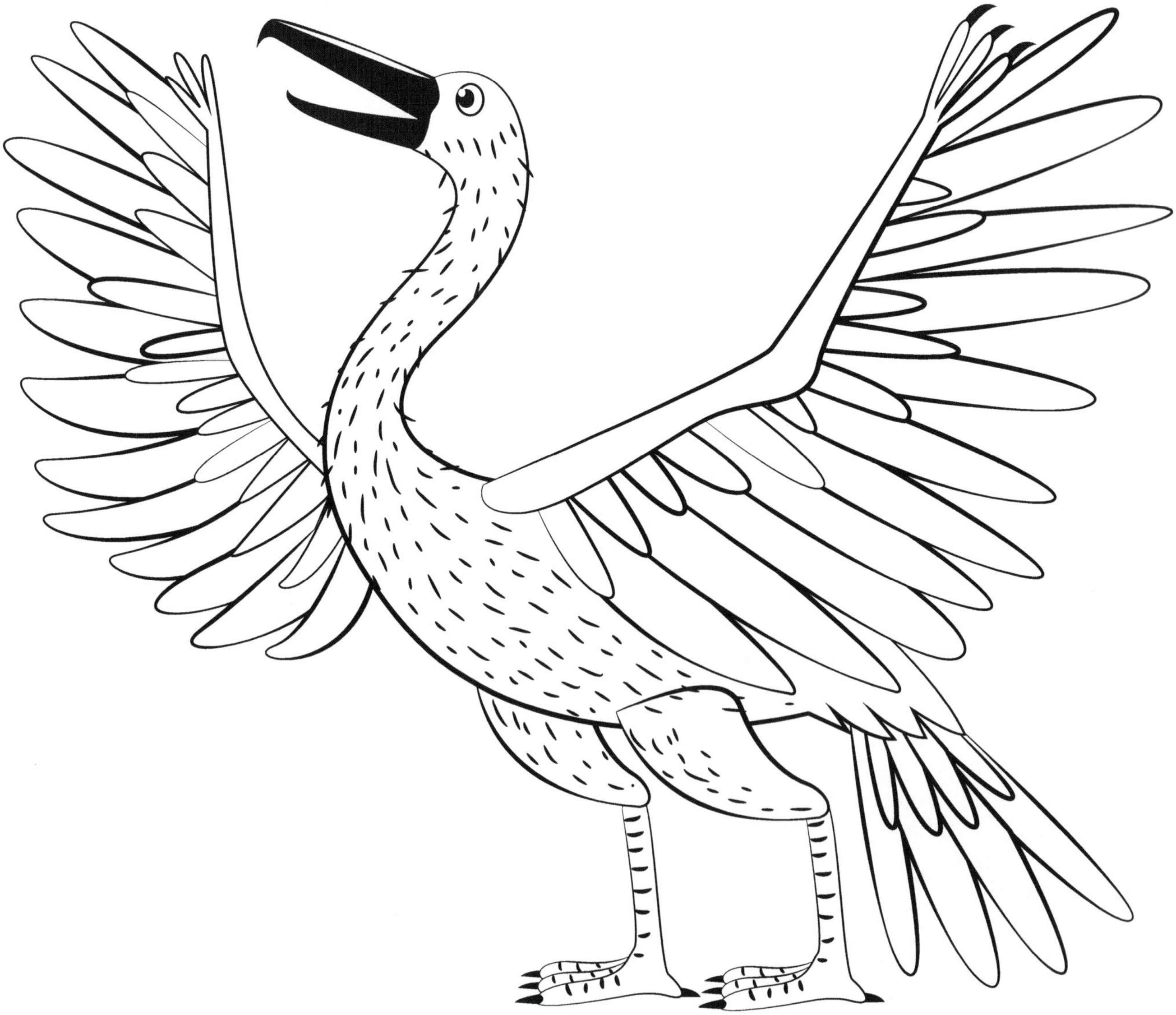

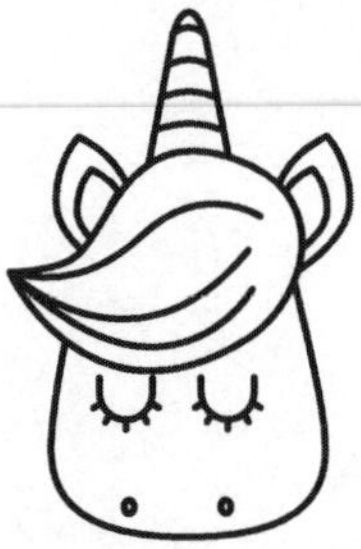

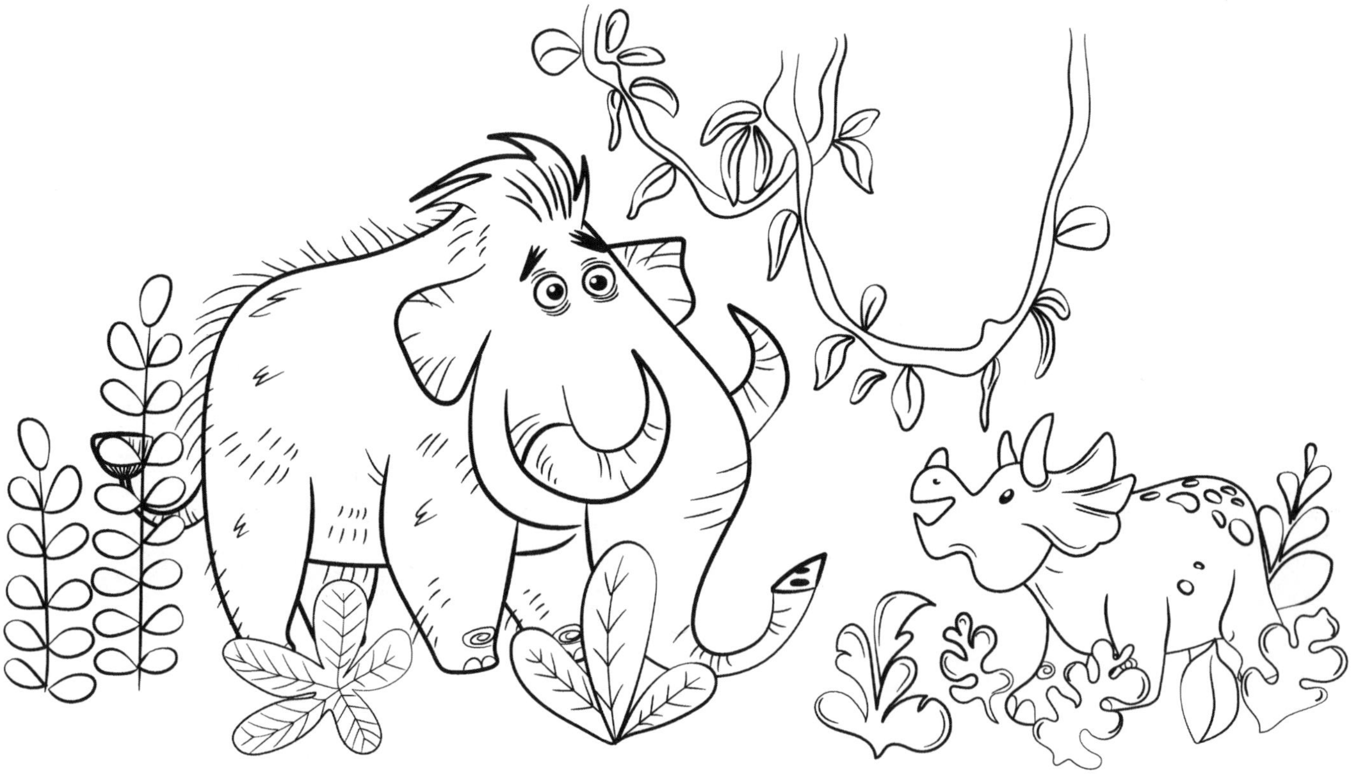

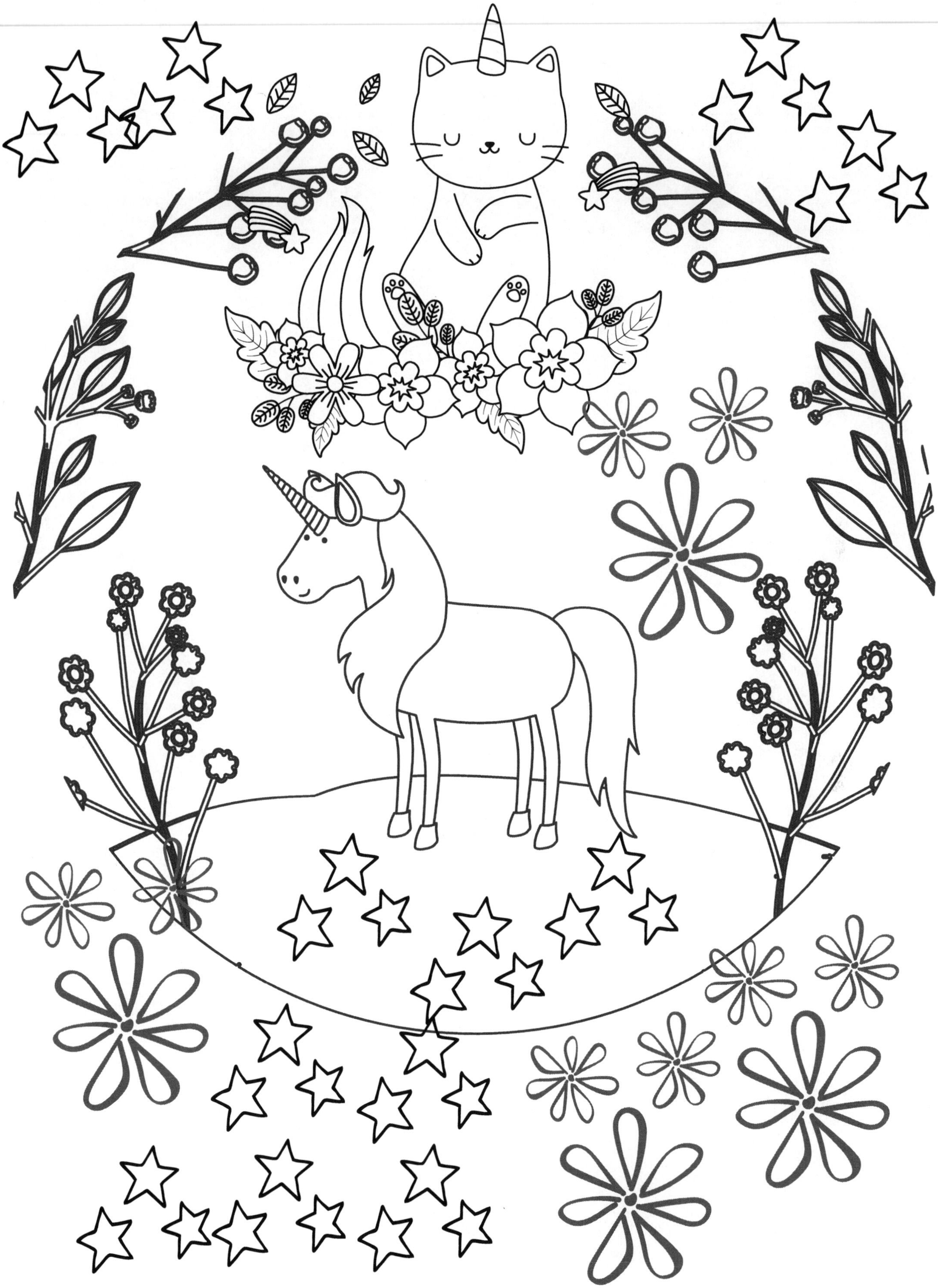

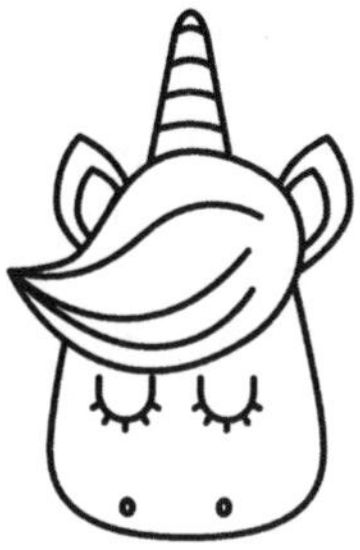

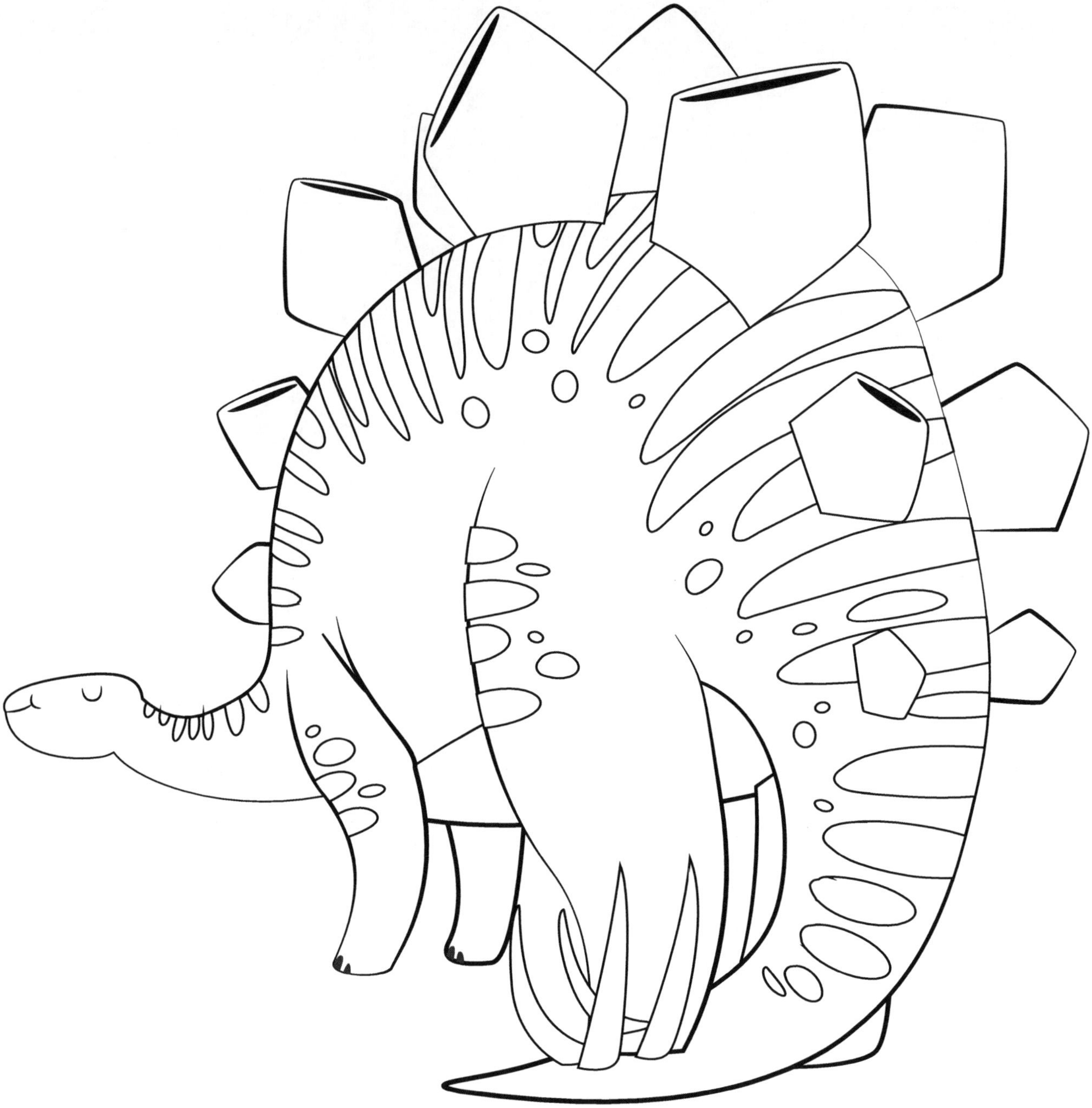

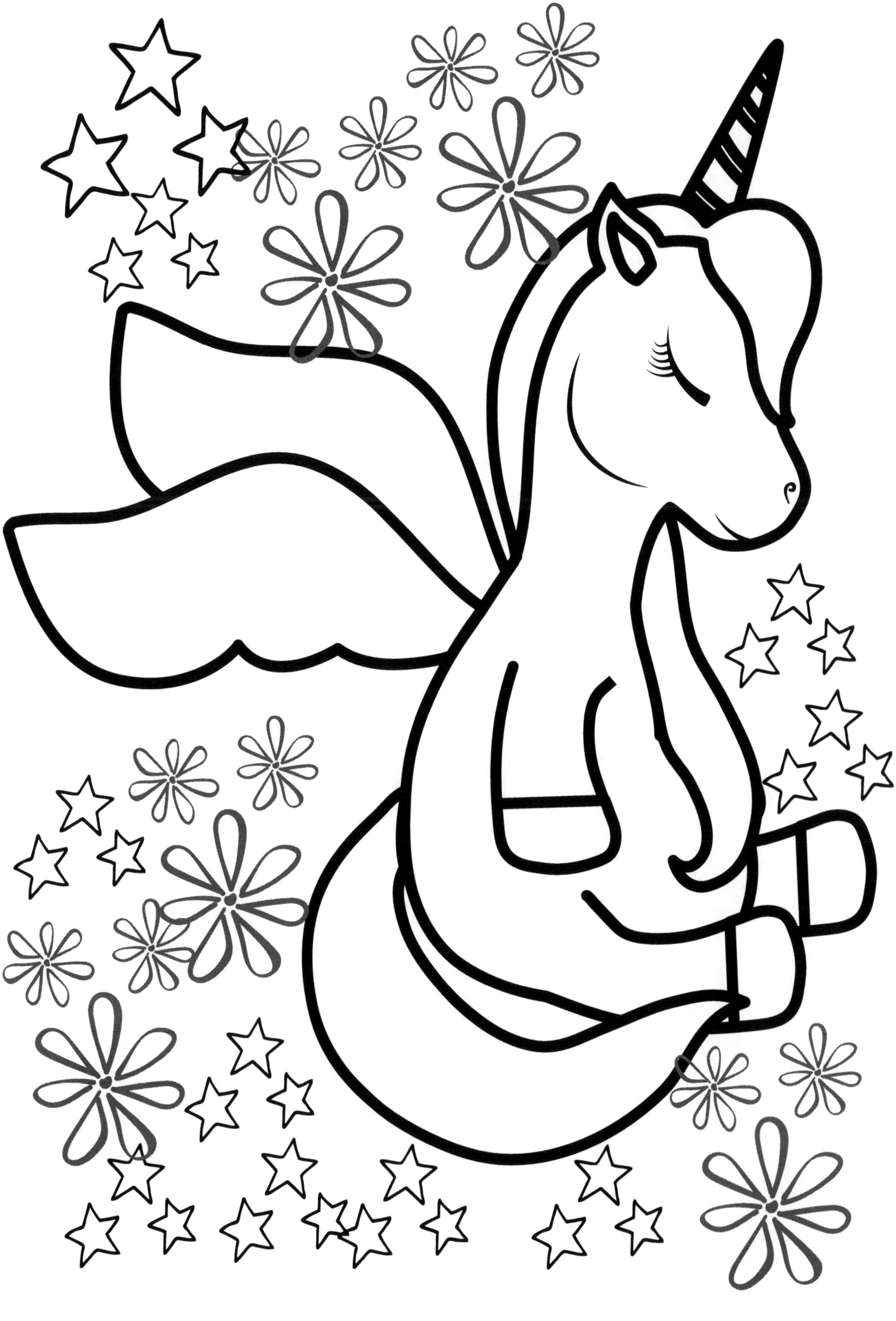

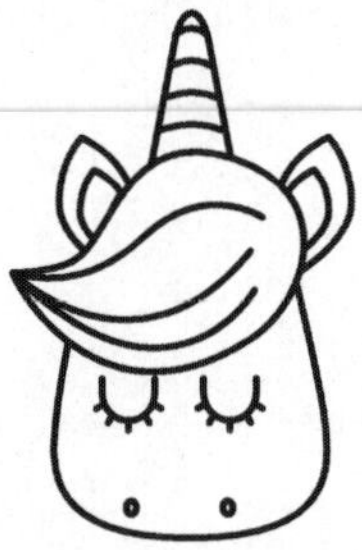

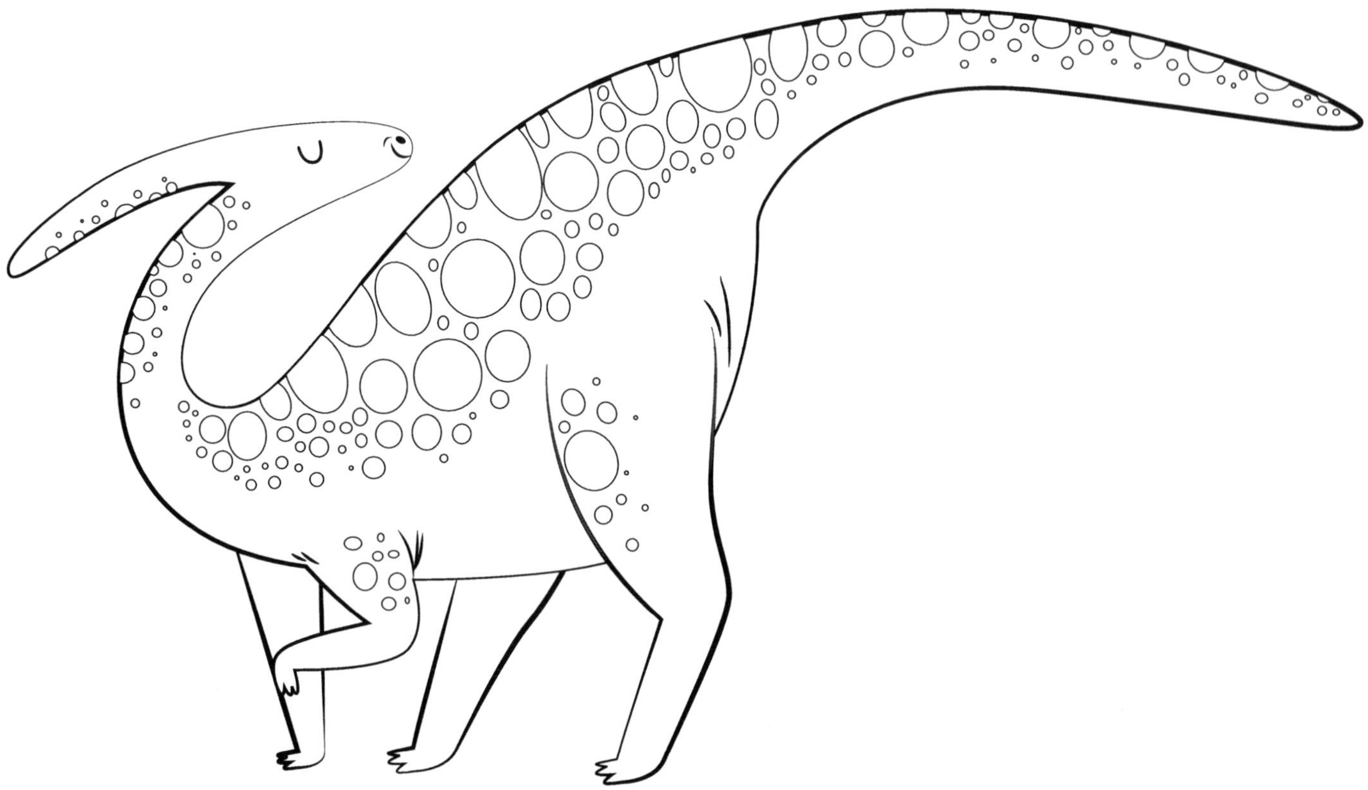

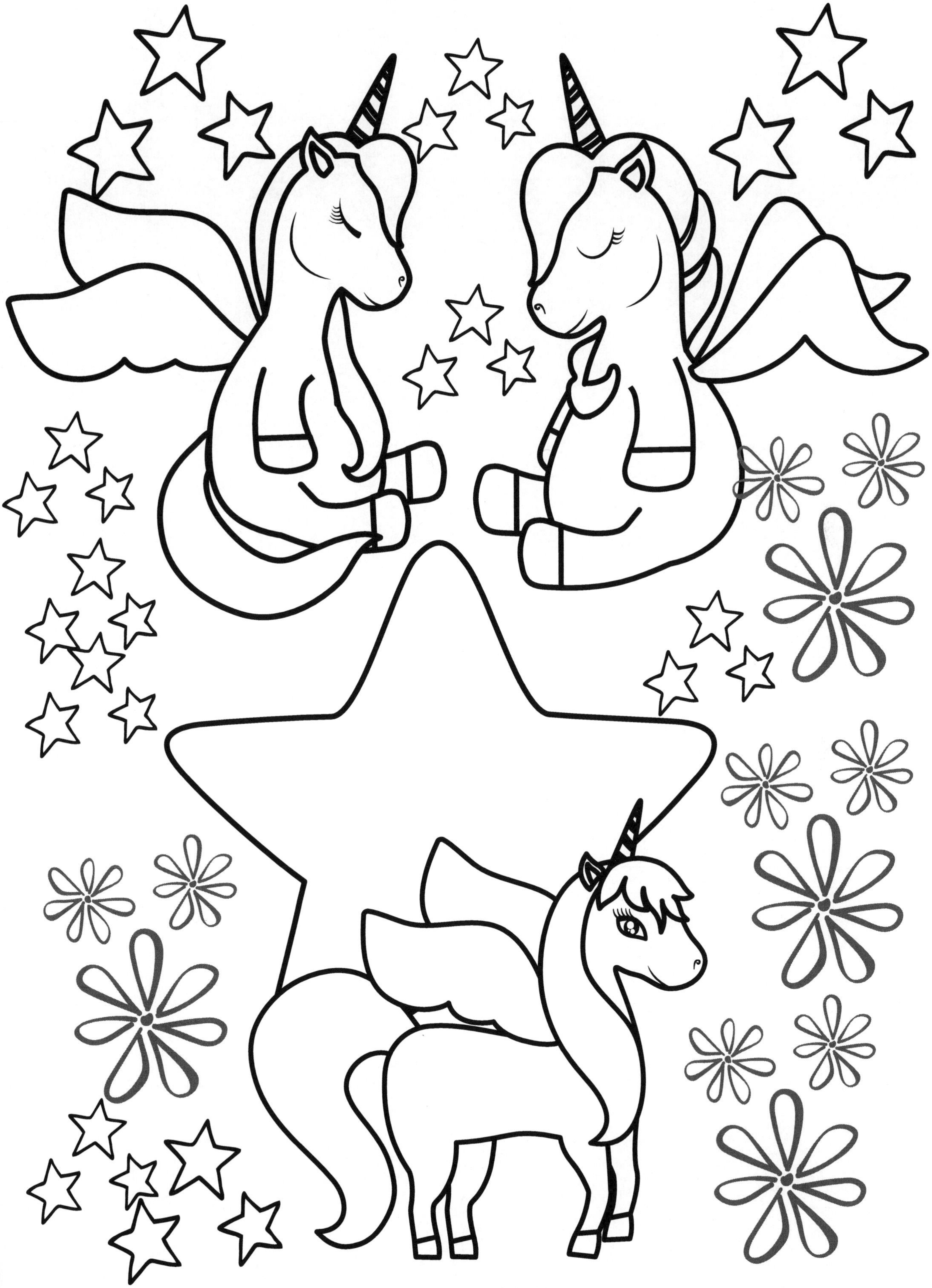

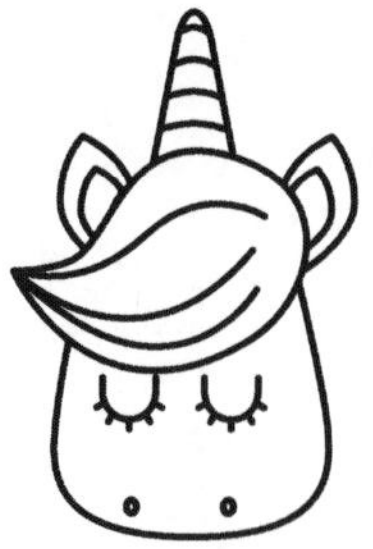

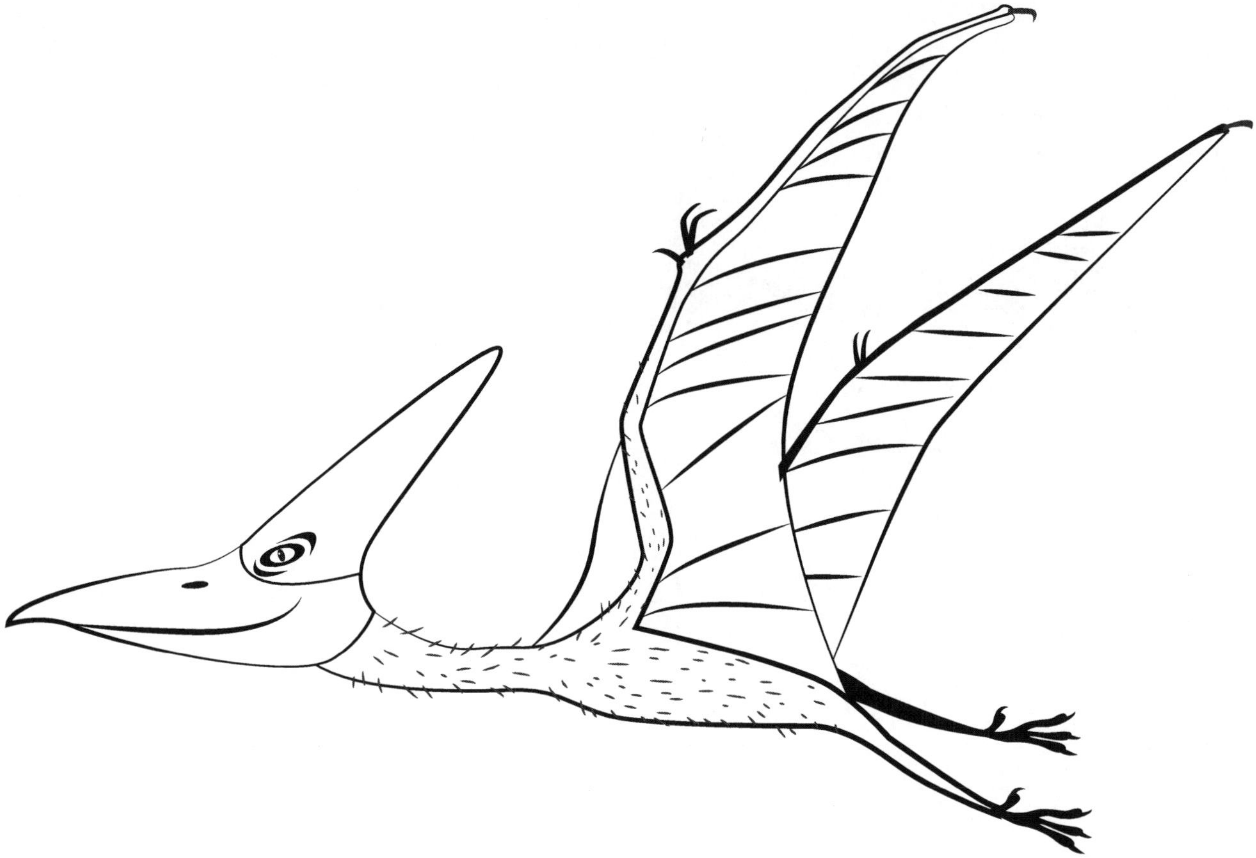

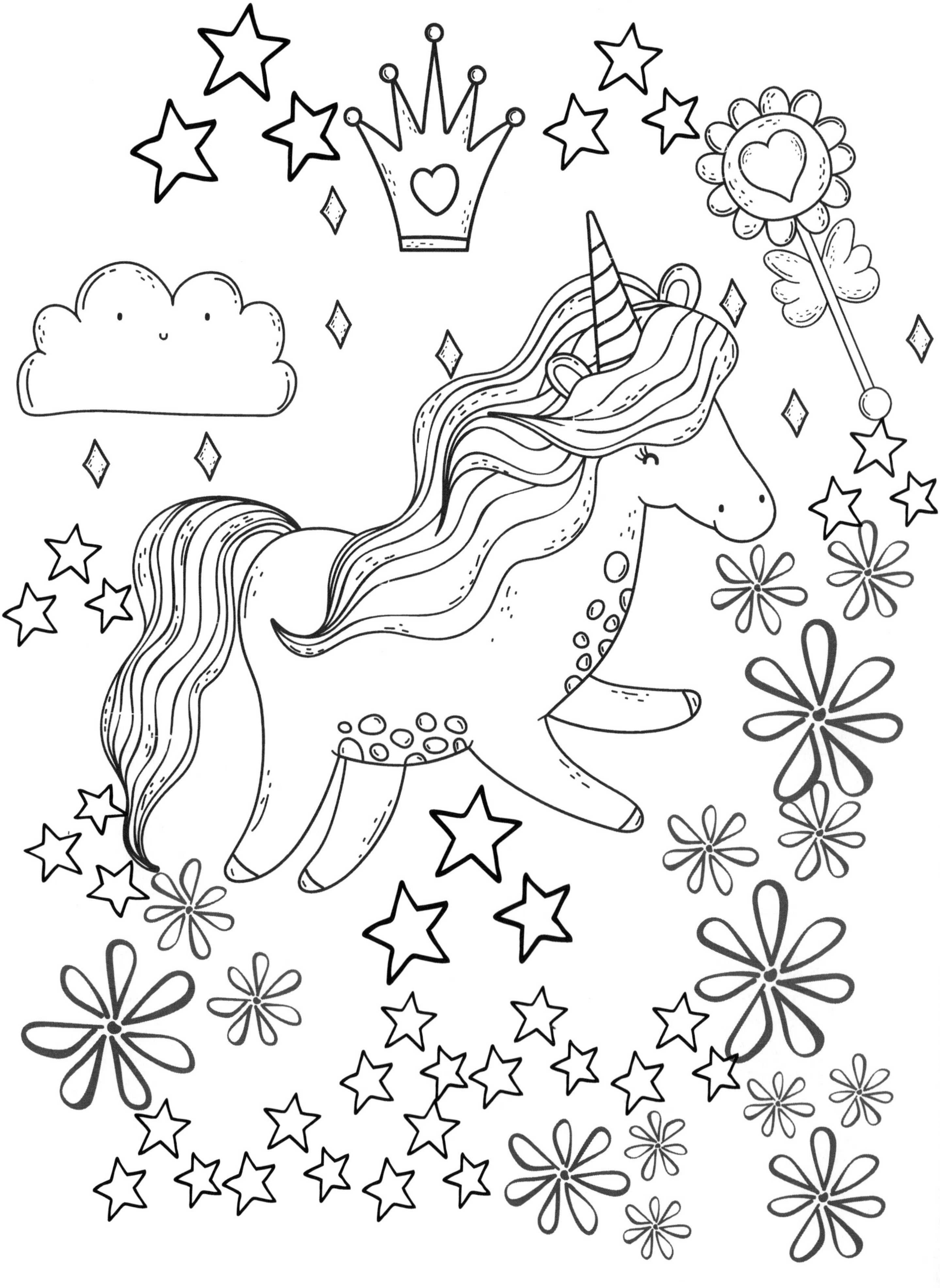

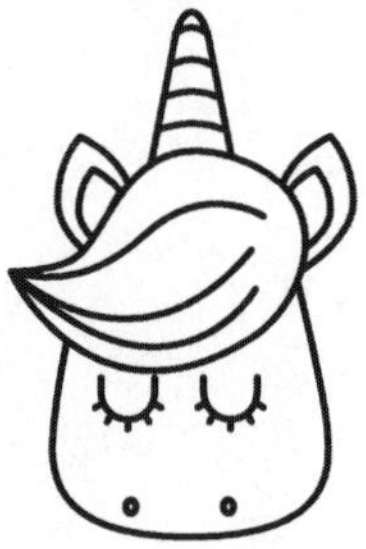

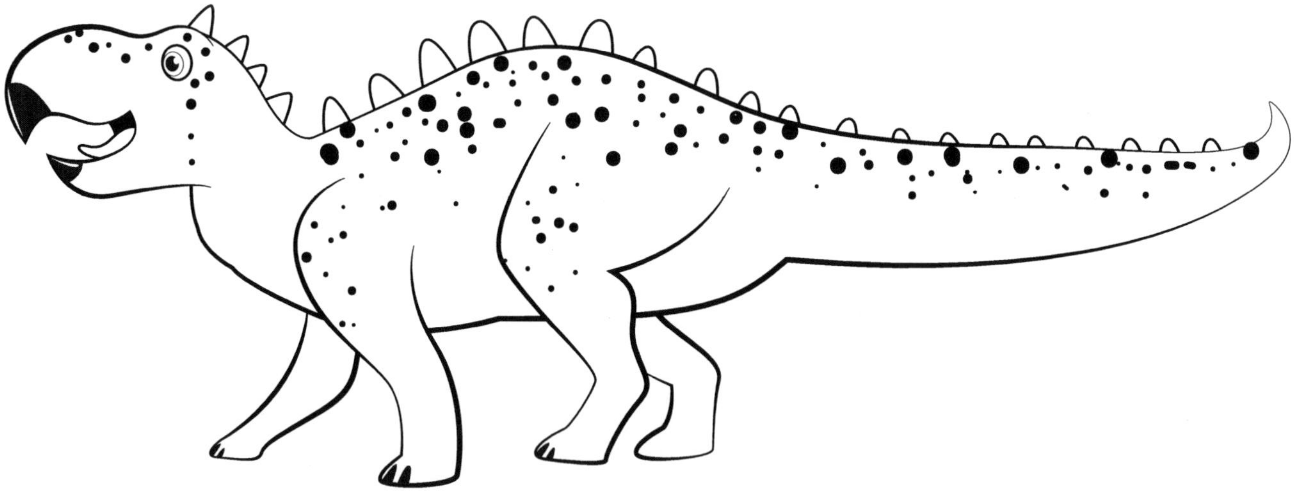

Made in the USA
Monee, IL
06 September 2021

77480579R00044